spiritual healing

 a beginner's guide

KRISTYNA ARCARTI

Headway · Hodder & Stoughton

Dedication

To Darren – a true friend and a ray of sunshine. Thanks for everything you do for me, for your help, your support, and your patience.

ISBN 0 340 674164

First published 1996
Impression number 10 9 8 7 6 5 4 3 2 1
Year   1999 1998 1997 1996

Typeset by Transet Limited, Coventry, England.
Printed in Great Britain for Hodder & Stoughton Educational, a division of Hodder Headline plc, 338 Euston Road, London NW1 3BH by Cox and Wyman Limited, Reading, Berks.

CONTENTS

INTRODUCTION

At some time or another, most of us will have need of healing. When we fall ill, a trip to the chemist, herbalist, homeopath and/or doctor will often put us on the right track again. Sometimes, the illness to which we fall foul will require more in-depth treatment, and prescription drugs will be given to us to enable us to recover, or it might even be necessary for us to receive hospital treatment. The purpose of this book is to show that there is another form of treatment which we could consider when we fall ill – that of spiritual healing. (Spiritual healing should not be confused with magnetic or pranic healing, or psychic healing, which are slightly different.)

Health is something which is of interest to us all, and I believe that good health is the right of us all. Unfortunately, that doesn't often prove to be the case. Many people, for no apparent reason, seem to suffer varying health problems throughout their lives. Others seem to get by with only a few minor hiccups en route. Still others, by virtue of their lifestyle, diet, character or attitude seem to attract more than their fair share of health problems.

Some sceptics would argue that spiritual healing achieves only a reduction of stress and thus an enhancement of the body's natural defence mechanisms. Others would suggest that hormones may be produced which have a beneficial effect on the function of organs and tissues, or that antibodies in the immune system are strengthened. They may also suggest that spiritual healing merely seeks to reinforce the mental attitude of patients so that they feel better in themselves. All of these opinions may be true, to a certain extent.

During the course of this book, we will take a look at healing in all its forms, but concentrate our thoughts on spiritual healing. Many people will automatically think of spiritual healing as a paranormal therapy,

and indeed it does sometimes fall into this category, along with faith healing, charismatic healing, absent healing, therapeutic touch and auric healing, all of which will be discussed later in this book.

There are many recorded examples of successful spiritual healing, and, where appropriate, examples will be given, but in this book I am not aiming to give detailed case histories.

ANOTHER 'NEW AGE' FAD?

During the past few years, there has been an increasing interest in methods of healing which involve outside forces, and many forms of complementary healing have grown in prominence. Not all forms of complementary therapy involve the use of herbs, needles or oils. Spiritual healing relies on natural powers, and is something which has been known to the human race for many centuries. Spiritual healing is, therefore, not a 'New Age' treatment, and indeed many forms of complementary healing are far from being new trends: aromatherapy, for example, can be traced back to the Egyptians, herbalism probably even further, and newer healing methods, such as Bach Flower Remedies have their origins in earlier treatments.

SPIRITUAL HEALING AS A COMPLEMENTARY TREATMENT

Even with the advances in technology and in medical research, and improvements in the drugs available to us, there is still an acute need for spiritual healing, as there is for all kinds of complementary healing. Irrespective of whether healing is administered by a spiritual healer, a general practitioner, herbalist, homeopath or whoever, it is the end result and the relief of suffering which should be the paramount concern, rather than the form of healing given.

It is, unfortunately, true that many, although not all, of the medical profession worldwide scoff at the idea that any form of healing other than their own can cause any improvement in a medical condition.

Those healers who practise outside of the medical profession are more likely to believe that all forms of healing are beneficial, and that there is nothing wrong at all with differing forms of healing running side by side. Spiritual healing, because of its very nature, will always be open to debate and discussion. It is also an unfortunate fact that many people will turn to spiritual healing only as a last resort, from a feeling of desperation, when all other avenues have been explored to their fullest.

Healing ourselves and others

In the following pages there is information and guidance on spiritual healing which can help everyone, irrespective of their religion or personal belief. We are all capable of helping to heal both each other and ourselves, although some people seem to be naturally gifted healers. However, we can all develop our healing gifts, and learn how to use them for self healing and to help other people.

I believe that all healing starts with self healing, and we will be discussing various methods of self healing during the course of this book. We will then move on to look at healing other people. We must feel well ourselves, be competent and confident at trying to heal our own health problems using the Universal Power of spiritual healing, before we launch into the mammoth task of healing other people.

The human race as a whole has a lot of potential. Learning to use our ability to heal properly may be one of the biggest single factors in improving our life on this planet, both for the present and for the future.

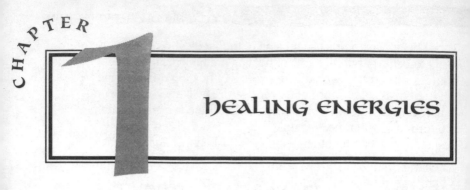

ḥEALING ENERGIES

I once read an article which contained the sentence 'Life is probably the greatest free gift we are ever likely to receive'. Indeed that is true, but there is more to life than just existing. We also have the gift of being able to improve our health, or to retain the level of health we already have.

You may feel that this is a sweeping statement and, at one time, I would have agreed with you. I was young, healthy and active, had a good well-paid job, and felt that ill health was something which either would never happen to me, or if it should, it certainly wouldn't change my way of life. It was only when I became ill that I began to realise that good health is an important component of a happy lifestyle. That is not to say that people who are ill are never happy, as many people who suffer with ill health are among the happiest in our society. Personally, I found that ill health meant that I was unable to do the things that I had done before with the same gusto and enthusiasm, and small tasks which I had previously done with little thought became insurmountable obstacles. It was during this time that I started to read more about healing – the types of healing available, what they entailed, where to find them, etc. Spiritual healing was one of the things I researched in depth, and being actively involved in a church which had a healing group, I went along to the healing services, firstly as an observer and later as a patient. During that time, and especially subsequently, I have seen people from all walks of life, with all sorts of illnesses go to see spiritual healers.

Spiritual healing in some cases is not a cure-all. It is not unusual for people to have spiritual healing and discover that an improvement in their condition is a slow process. Unfortunately, miracles don't

often happen, although there are still some people whose cases are reported in the media who do find immediate cures. In most cases, however, the improvement in health takes time. Sadly, the majority of media reporting of spiritual healing focuses on the unpredictability of the success rate, and scientific tests often serve to undermine the whole process. For spiritual healing to be successful, it is important that patient and healer are attuned not only to each other, but to the healing energies. If there is an imbalance or lack of attunement, the healing energies will not flow so freely. Often in test situations there is a great deal of tension and stress and so, obviously, the healing energies will flow less freely. However, if you try to explain that to the media, you will probably find them quoting your 'excuse' for lack of success, rather than explaining the reason for it.

At this stage it is worthwhile pointing out that another explanation as to why spiritual healing isn't always successful may lie with the healer him or herself. It takes many years of work and preparation to be an effective healer, and these things cannot be rushed. Many times, those who feel they have something to offer in the field of spiritual healing launch themselves on the public without the necessary experience, knowledge or ability. Healers need to have high standards; much is expected of them, and it is only fair that the help that they give matches the expectations of their patients.

Wbat is spiritual Ժealing?

The first thing you should appreciate about spiritual healing is that it is not a miracle treatment, and it may also not provide a complete cure for an illness or medical condition. Not everybody can or will be cured, and you should realise from the outset that there is a wealth of difference between healing and curing. In spiritual healing, which is basically the channelling of powers from a source higher than ourselves for the benefit of the patient concerned, there will be, in most cases, an improvement in the condition being treated, but how much improvement will depend on the individual, as well as how advanced the disease may be at the time of the initial consultation.

Unfortunately, many people turn to spiritual healing as a last resort, when their disease is well advanced, and this often means that the healing given cannot be as effective. In such cases, the best that can be achieved may be a reduction in the pain being experienced.

In an attempt to understand spiritual healing, many people will start to wonder where the powers originate. Those people who have a belief in God may suggest that the healing power comes from God Himself. Those who do not believe in God will point to shamen of many cultures and suggest that the power comes from Nature or from spirits. At the end of the day, irrespective of where the power to heal originates, it exists, and is something which can help each and every one of use at some time or another, should we choose to allow it.

There are many theories put forward by practitioners of spiritual healing, all attempting to explain what they do and how their healing works, but in truth, the answer is that we really don't know. Some people will suggest that the healing treatment is only a matter of faith. The power of the mind, which we will discuss in greater detail later, is a strong force, and remission in an illness can be triggered or lengthened, or the illness may indeed be halted, by the power of the mind. Followers of New Age and Eastern philosophies, who understand about chakra centres (energy centres) and the aura (the energy field which surrounds each person), will argue that the healer has been able to alter the body's energy field to bring an improvement, each cell in the body being its own energy source, much like a little battery. Those people who understand about acupuncture and reflexology will be aware of the energy channels within the body, and how manipulation of these channels can bring about relief of pain or reduction in symptoms in another part of the body entirely.

I have already explained how those who have a belief in God will suggest that they are merely channelling powers from The Creator, which are available for us all to use and to tap into, should we have the skill to do so. Other people who carry out healing works, and not only those who follow shamanistic practices, will suggest that an intermediary is involved, such as a deceased person, quite often a doctor or someone who worked in a healing capacity when alive, or even from deceased relatives or ancestors, and that the healing powers are coming from that source.

I would categorise those healers who claim to work with discarnate
entities as psychic healers, rather than spiritual healers. Those who
use their own psychic powers or enlist the help of the spirit world
are using either their own energies or those of another human, albeit
someone who has passed on, rather than using the power of The
Creator, or of the universe. Likewise, those healers practising
magnetic or pranic healing are also in the main part using their own
personal energies. I would suggest that healing power is inherent in
all of us, should we know how to tap into it, and that it comes from
an energy greater than we ourselves are or ever could aspire to
become. If you want to call that power 'God', then that's fine. The
problem of using your own energies to help in the healing process is
that the powers are limited to the healer him or herself. I have tried
to heal using magnetic healing, and I ended up feeling totally
depleted of my own personal energy, having transferred everything I
have to the other party. As a result, healing in this way limits the
amount of people you can endeavour to help, and you can also run
yourself down in the process. Spiritual healing, because it taps into
a power source other than your own personal energy system, does
not run into these problems.

Explaining how spiritual healing works is a complicated process,
open to a lot of sceptical argument. Sometimes it is all too easy to
try to over-analyse something in an attempt to understand it, and
you may wonder if it is really necessary to know why something
works. If something works, perhaps that is all we need to understand.

HEALING POWERS

Spiritual healing is all about tapping into the power available to us
all to help us to improve our health, should we fall ill. Maybe that is
all we need to understand. In addition to an outer power, there are
our own inner powers which we can harness at times of illness to
help bring about an improvement in condition and a return to good
health. These are seemingly two separate systems, but they share a
common link, that of energy, and I am referring here not to our own

body energy systems, but to something on a grander scale. Let's start to think about this power in a form which we can understand – electricity.

Most of us have electricity in our homes. Electricity is an energy, a power, which is available both to us personally within our homes and also in the world at large. When we press our light switch, the light comes on. The power to light the bulb comes from the electricity system available to us, which feeds into our houses by means of cables. We don't see these cables, unless we are around when they are being installed, but nevertheless, we know that they are there, somewhere. Sometimes, however, we press our light switch and the light doesn't come on. We don't then assume that there is a problem with the electric grid, but look closer to home at the light bulb or at the fuse box. We are fortunate that the electric supply is available to us, for no matter how many times we put in a new light bulb or check the fuses, the light won't come on if the supply isn't there, these two things being linked. Fortunately for us, the power we need to tap into to heal ourselves and others is there for us all the time. Both the power without and the power within come from the same ultimate source. One is external to us, the other is internal and involves us and our lives.

Now let's go back to our bodies, and the healing energies which we can use. Spiritual healing involves transference of energy from an outer source into the body as a whole, or to a specific area of the body, to bring about healing. It also involves regenerating energies already present within cells of the body which may be impaired or reduced in efficiency. Sometimes this healing is carried out by personal touch or similar one-to-one healing treatments; at other times, this is carried out at a distance.

There have been many experiments undertaken in the latter part of the twentieth century which have set out to show what happens during the transference of energy in spiritual healing: whether it is so vitally important for the healing to be by laying-on of hands, or by therapeutic touch (discussed at length later), or whether the healing energies can be tapped into and transferred over distance, by what is known as absent healing.

Absent healing can be carried out with or without the help of the patient concerned. Sometimes the healer works alone, and sometimes within a group, but while the patient takes no active part, the patient should be in a relaxed state so that he or she is more receptive to the healing energies. Absent healing is especially useful in cases where a patient is too ill to travel.

There has always been the need to put to scientific test claims made for any complementary therapy, and spiritual healing is no different. Many tests have been undertaken in the United States, and one famous test case on transferring energy was carried out in the late 1960s. Two healers, Ambrose and Olga Worrell, were asked by Dr Robert Miller to test whether their healing abilities could affect the speed of growth in grass seeds. The healers, who were 600 miles away from the laboratories at the time, concentrated their healing energies on the task at hand, with the amazing result that the grass, the normal growth of which was around two millimetres per day, grew to more than a centimetre. Ambrose and Olga Worrall firmly believed that they were channels for a universal energy originating with God and that, because spiritual healing is a natural process, working in harmony with natural laws, it can be accomplished over long distances. During such healing sessions, Ambrose Worrall said he felt energy leaving him through his solar plexus.

Around the same time, similar experiments on the growth of barley plants carried out by biochemist Doctor Justa Smith and Hungarian healer Oskar Estebany showed similar success. Further work undertaken by Dr Smith and Mr Estebany showed that he was able to restore to health enzymes which had been damaged by exposure to ultraviolet light in a way which resembled the improvement shown when the damaged enzymes were brought into a high magnetic field. It became clear that the healing process tapped into an energy, that the healer 'tuned in' to this energy, and thus the healing process began. Further experiments attempting to measure the amount of 'energy' produced have not been successful, possibly because the world is not familiar with this type of energy.

In the late 1980s, similar experiments in healing were carried out at London University by Dr David Hodges and Dr Tony Scofield. They

tested a healer who claimed he was able to increase the growth of cress seeds which had been hampered by soaking in salt water overnight. The healer actually held some of the seeds for a short time, and directed healing energies to them, while other seeds were left untouched. It was shown that the seeds which the healer had held grew at a faster rate than those which he had not, and so it was concluded that the healer did transmit a healing energy which enabled the seeds to grow normally.

Tests on people rather than on plants have included heart-disease patients and migraine sufferers. In the United States, patients were treated by spiritual healers and by actors claiming to be healers, while actually concentrating on something else. In the tests, the genuine treatments gave significantly better improvements, and similar tests on patients suffering with rheumatoid arthritis have been carried out more recently in the United Kingdom in Leeds.

Thinking about illnesses

I consider illness, or disease, to be a dis-ease or lack of ease of parts of the body with the whole, and firmly believe in holistic therapies. Illness is an interruption of the harmony of the body structure, a depletion or imbalance of energies within the body. What the healer is trying to do is to reintroduce energy by acting as a channel for that energy, so that the natural harmony and balance of the body can be restored, and it will no longer be at dis-ease with itself. Because at the time of the healing treatment, as we will discuss later, the healer's mind and the mind of the patient are already in harmony, the energy is able to be transferred through to the patient at a deeper level than would occur otherwise.

I firmly believe that if you think positively and 'think well' your health can improve, even if only marginally. Negative thoughts and beliefs can, and do, have a strong effect on health, and we will discuss the power of the mind in greater detail later. However, it is important to understand from the beginning that your body can be run down easily by overworking your mind. I always try to live in a

peaceful and calm state of existence as much as possible, even though, at times, that seems totally impossible, and I have to get away from home base to totally relax.

Many illnesses in our modern world are caused by inadequate diet, poor lifestyle habits and negative thinking. I realise that what I am about to explain can prove to be a difficult and testing experiment, but it is well worth the effort. Next time you are faced with someone who is obviously tense, angry or stressed, try to remain totally calm yourself, unaffected by their demeanour, and see how your state of calm will ultimately transfer itself across to the other party, and notice how the state of tension will subside. You may wish to have something to focus your mind upon to help this process, and you can try various things from a beautiful rose to something more personal to you and/or the person with whom you are interacting. I try to concentrate on the colour pink, which I feel to be the colour of unconditional love, and imagine that pink colour permeating the very pores of the other person.

Irrespective of what visualisation technique you choose to consider, how much better for everybody to try to do something to reduce tensions both in ourselves and in others, and thereby avoid unnecessary stresses and strains on our bodies. At some time, we all need to step outside ourselves, relax and calm ourselves in order to operate effectively.

If we could all try just a little harder to stop ourselves reaching a state of tension by letting situations wash over us without causing too much damage, we would all, perhaps, be a lot healthier.

Thinking Þolistically

Spiritual healing is about treating the body and mind as a unit, as healing affects body, mind and emotions. As with other forms of holistic treatment, spiritual healing does not segment one part of the body from another. If part of the body is unwell, it will affect the whole person, and thus the whole body will be subject to the healing process, not just the part of the body causing problems. Likewise,

spiritual healing does not confine itself to mere body parts. It also encompasses the mental and emotional aspects of the person, acknowledging the connection between the mind and the body. Occasionally, in order to supplement the healing process, special diets are also suggested.

Good health can have a lot to do with a person's attitude, emotions and abilities to be positive. Negativities, the state of being continuously anxious and worried, can have a detrimental effect on the body and make situations worse. A little anxiety and tension is good for us, and is necessary for the body to work effectively, but all too often, we are subject to a lot of stress and tension which in turn creates more anxieties, worries and depressions. It is also fair to say that a negative attitude on the part of doctors and other people generally can contribute to a general state of negativity for many patients. Likewise, what is known as 'a good bedside manner' will help a patient feel cheerful and recovery may be accelerated as a result. Basically, the patient will relax, and relaxation on the part of both the healer and the patient is most important for a successful healing. Often a healer who tries too hard to help a patient will in turn become tense, and this tension will transmit itself to the person undergoing healing, and little will be achieved. In addition to the element of relaxation, the healer must feel genuine compassion and love for the patient, and sincerely wish to see that person's health improve. We will discuss the power of love in a later chapter.

faith, belief and the placebo effect

There will always be those who will query whether spiritual healing works or not, and why it will work on some people and not so well on others. We have already briefly discussed some reasons for this, and others will be put forward as we progress. Sceptics will argue that the lack of total success is a direct result of lack of faith on the part of the patient – all the successes are really down to a matter of

faith or belief, rather than something more tangible and real. In answer to this, I would point out that spiritual healing can be practised on animals as well as on human beings, and even though an animal may be appreciative of concern shown towards it, it cannot have faith in a spiritual sense, yet the healing will still take place. Surely, then, faith really doesn't enter into the equation too much. Obviously, if there is a belief in the healing powers, the chances are that the healing will take place at a faster rate, but faith really isn't the primary force. Healing isn't faith, it is merely channelling power for the good of humanity as a whole.

When thinking in terms of faith and healing, one normally conjures up pictures of evangelical faith-healing services, where the highly charged atmosphere can often seem to bring about a remarkable improvement in a patient's condition. Unfortunately, this improvement rarely lasts, as such instant results are normally due to an elevated state of mind rather than an improvement in bodily symptoms. Spiritual healing is not faith healing, but a totally separate thing, although like spiritual healing and other forms of healing therapy, faith healing has existed throughout history. It seemed to undergo a revival in the late nineteenth and early twentieth centuries with evangelistic healers like Oral Roberts, Kathryn Kuhlman and Jack Coe becoming celebrities in the field, especially in the United States, and faith healing is still an integral part of the Pentecostal Church. Healing also forms part of the work of many other religious groups.

Belief is a slightly different entity to faith. Belief in yourself and your abilities can be utilised in many forms, and often leads to people fulfilling their expectations in career, relationships, etc. Belief that a healing treatment will work can play an important role in how quickly the healing effects take place. It is widely accepted by both the medical profession and layworkers in the field of health that bodily functions such as blood pressure and heart rate can be open to personal influence. Biofeedback techniques have supported this in test situations, and likewise those people who study or practise meditation will be well aware that they can and do lower their heart rates when meditating.

Experiments into varying types of meditation technique undertaken in the 1960s by Lawrance LeShan, a psychologist, showed that while in a meditative state, those who were observing him noticed physical and psychological changes which also benefitted them, and it was discovered that he could actually teach others how to meditate and awaken their own healing powers.

In the field of hypnosis, readers may probably be aware of the work done in England in the early 1950s by Dr Mason, who succeeded in curing a patient of ichthyosis (a skin disease previously thought incurable) by suggesting under hypnosis that the condition would be cured. The development of hypnotism is said to have actually come about as a result of the work carried out in the eighteenth century by Franz Anton, more commonly known as Mesmer (hence Mesmerism). A student of medicine, Mesmer experimented with magnetic healing, using a baquet (a round wooden bathtub filled with magnetised water), and later discovered that he could transmit healing through touch as well, using the transference of energies.

Obviously, belief played a great part in these healing treatments, and this leads us on to the placebo effect. For those who are unaware of the meaning of this term, the placebo effect has been demonstrated worldwide in various tests over various timespans, and is basically an improvement in condition following the administration of certain pills or medications (normally sugar based) which, in fact, are inert and contain no active ingredients. The patient believes the medication contains drugs which will aid his or her medical condition. In addition, the person prescribing the treatment will endeavour to come across as all-knowing, caring and attentive, thus boosting the patients belief that the medication is the best possible treatment. The actual word 'placebo' comes from the Latin for 'I will please'.

It is fair to say that over the last few years, tests have shown beyond a doubt that at least 35 per cent of patients respond successfully to the placebo, and sometimes there has even been a complete recovery by the patient.

The suggestion then is that the patient's belief in the power of the medication has brought about the cure, in much the same way as those who have religious beliefs will suggest that the patient has

been cured by his or her own faith. The argument will suggest that the placebo, and/or the faith or belief, has acted as a sort of catalyst or focus of attention which has served to activate the body to heal itself. Following that train of thought, sceptics of spiritual healing will point to the success rate of psychotherapy, hypnotherapy, regressive therapy and the like, and it is only right to acknowledge that there is no way of registering what part belief plays in the success of any treatment. Many good results obtained by spiritual healing are ascribed by the medical profession to a temporary lifting in mental attitude, and it is worthwhile pointing out that most spiritual healers will not tell a patient he or she is incurable, as it will encourage that patient to think negatively. Unfortunately, spiritual healing is often sought as a last resort, when the body is already under attack from which it cannot recover, but spiritual healing will, at the very least, have a positive psychological effect and a patient can be relieved of stress and tension.

Many illnesses, as we have discussed, can and do start with mental stresses and strains, and many illnesses can be shown to have psychosomatic origins, and similarly many diseases can be accelerated by negative or pessimistic thinking. It is very easy to give in to negative thoughts, especially when receiving a diagnosis which is not favourable, and when this happens there is a marked deterioration, in many cases, in both the condition and attitude of the patient concerned.

In the United States, there has been a great deal of work carried out into negative thought patterns, and it has been proven in tests undertaken by Dr Carl Simonton in Texas that the reintroduction of positive thoughts can completely reverse the downward spirals. On a personal level, I know that positivity can help. My husband was told he was terminally ill in the October of a particular year and that he would not live to see the beginning of December because the cancer he had was far too advanced. He failed to accept this, said that he was determined to be at home and well enough to enjoy Christmas, and lived to do just that. His willpower and determination carried him through. Scientists will acknowledge that those people who survive terminal illnesses the longest, sometimes by at least fifteen years, were those people who refused to accept that they

were expected to die shortly and had the will to live, while those who resign themselves to dying will die far more quickly.

Outside Western culture, there are those who actively seek to inject negative beliefs on others, and there are many tales of death curses and hexes being dealt out by witch doctors, for example. In Australia, it is thought by the Aborigines that 'pointing the bone' at intended victims will bring about ill health, and it is fair to say that in any society, if you suggest negative things, they will be absorbed. We will discuss mental attitude in greater depth in a later chapter.

Thinking of healing ourselves

As we have seen, it is possible for us to help to heal ourselves with spiritual healing. In fact, the body usually heals itself, even if we are not consciously aware of the fact. For example, if you cut yourself opening a can, you would immediately wash the wound, probably put a plaster over it, and carry on with whatever you were doing. In a couple of days, when you take the plaster off, the bleeding will have stopped and the wound will have healed, or at least gone some way towards being completely healed. We take our body's ability to heal for granted, but it happens all the time. A similar thing happens following surgical operations, when the body will heal itself, even if part of it has been removed.

Let's take another example. The body has an immune system, which fights off infections, viruses and diseases. Sometimes, when our immune system is low, we will fall foul of say a cold, while at other times everybody around us will seem to be ill with coughs and colds, and we will remain immune to the virus. It is also worth pointing out that we all develop cancerous cells at some point during our lives, and normally a healthy immune system will spring into action and the diseased cells will be attacked and destroyed. Yet again, this happens without our conscious knowledge or effort. Medical research has learnt how to harness this system to develop drugs that

contain bacteria which, when introduced to the body, will strengthen the immune system and thus help the fight against illness. However, again we come back to the power of the mind, as it has proven in many cases that our immune system can be altered by our thoughts and feelings.

Some people, however, really do not wish to be well. There are people I know who can honestly be said to 'enjoy' bad health, especially those who feel that attention, love and affection is missing from their lives. They may even find themselves actively courting illness, and embracing it wholeheartedly when it comes along, as it is a means of allowing them to receive the attention and care they feel that they are lacking at other times. There is a medical condition known as Münchausen's disease which sees people claiming to have an imaginary illness in order to obtain hospital treatment. By the strength of mind power they can convince themselves of their ill health, and are able to produce symptoms of the illness. On a slightly less profound scale, there are others who may exaggerate a bona fide illness with the intention of making family and friends show how much they care, or just to offload something, like a job they don't want to do. All these people will fail to respond to spiritual healing, because they don't want to see an improvement, for whatever reason.

Before your body can start to heal itself, you should be as relaxed as possible. It is very easy to say that you should try to take time out each day to sit and relax. Many of us just don't have the chance to do that. Even if we try to sit down and relax, our minds will wander, and we will notice little jobs which need doing, or conversely feel selfish because we are ignoring the demands of our family. However, we do need to think of ourselves, and starting to relax is a good way of starting to understand what healing is all about.

Before starting to read the next chapter, take time out to sit or even to lie down on something comfortable, covering yourself to make sure that you don't feel cold, close your eyes, make yourself comfortable and just concentrate on breathing, Make sure that you will be free from distractions – take the telephone off the hook, and pick a time when you know everybody else you live with is out, and

just relax. Try to sit without crossing legs or arms, so that the energies you have within your body can flow unhindered. Bring your shoulders up to your ears, squeeze them tightly, and then let them fall. Do that a few times, taking deep breaths in when you bring your shoulders up, and letting your breath out with the fall of your shoulders. You may want something to visualise, so that your mind does not wander. Choose your own item. I normally choose a pink rose. Concentrate your mind on that object. If you wish to have background music, choose something soothing, preferably instrumental so that your mind does not dwell on any words. Let your body and mind relax until the end of one track of music. When the music has finished, have a little stretch, don't jump up and get going again. Take your time, acclimatise yourself to your surroundings, and then go about affairs rejuvenated. You have now gone a small way towards self-healing.

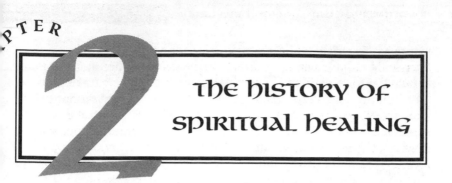

the history of spiritual healing

*W*e have already established that spiritual healing is not a new thing, so this chapter will concentrate on tracing the roots of healing in all its forms and look at its development, from the earliest records through to the present time.

healing in ancient civilisations

A common belief is that spiritual healing had its roots in biblical times or in ancient Egypt, Greece and Asia, but healing and healers go back even further than these large civilisations. Looking towards the original tribes of peoples who inhabited the globe, we have information to hand that these tribes had people within them who acted as healers. Obviously records were not kept by such people, so it is impossible to pinpoint accurately which tribes had which healers and so on, but it would be fair to say that the shamen, witch doctors and medicine men of various cultures which have managed to survive into the present time most probably have existed in that culture from earliest times. The types of healing prominent in early civilisations may not have been what we understand today by the term 'spiritual healing', but we will take a look at various cultures in an attempt to understand more about healing as a concept.

All over the globe, people in past civilisations have practised spiritual healing. One such group still in existence are the Huna of Hawaii, who actively practise holistic spiritual healing, taking into account not only physical causes, but emotional problems, attitudes and thoughts, feeling that healing involves working with the subconscious. There are similar counterparts in Tahiti and New Zealand, as well as other areas of the Pacific.

In Africa, the medicine man was most often a herbalist, but in East Africa, he was also a seller of charms and talismen to ward off illness and evil spirits. In Southern and Central Africa, the Nganga or medicine man was trained by his family, learning about herbs, roots, bark and flowers. Also recorded are instances of cures being passed on by dreams about ancestors, who gave the Nganga details of how to prepare the herbal remedies for the best type of cure.

In the North American Indian tradition, there have always been those who acted as healer for the tribe, in addition to which there was and still is the medicine wheel, which is a method of healing using a circle of rocks laid out on the ground, in the centre of which the Indians sit to draw power into their bodies. The healer within the tribe carries a bag of secret tools, included in which are a tiny sack of curative herbs, and it is interesting to note that the US Pharmacopeia and the National Formulary officially accepted 170 Indian drugs for their medicinal value. Most often, the healer offers a series of prayers or chants in an attempt to help the healing process, believing in one god and asking for his help and guidance. Healing ceremonies carried out by the Indian people almost always include chanting (known as Chantways). Similarly chanting often accompanies other healing ceremonies carried out by various religious and non-religious groups and organisations. These will be discussed in a later chapter.

Shamanic Healing

Many readers may be new to the word 'shamen', and it is important to understand exactly what shamen are and were.

Shamen is a term which, especially today, is applied to many sorts of people, from healers, medicine men and mystics through to sorcerers and magicians, but in history, shamen within any group or civilisation were considered to be storytellers and magicians, those who often sang magical songs. The word 'shamen' may come from a word *saman* used in Siberia and Central Asia, or conversely from the Sanskrit word *saman* meaning 'song'.

Shamen appear in the North American Indian tradition, as well as in the Australian Aborigines, and followers of various pagan organisations will also have people within their group known as shamen. In order to distinguish themselves from the group, and as a sign of authority, shamen wear special garments.

While a shaman may use meditation to bring about a state of altered consciousness, the shaman may also, through songs and chants, aim to contact spirits and communicate with them. The main function, however, of a shaman is that of healing. Shamanism in its purist form makes no differential between body, mind and spirit, and diagnosis of an illness is made by consultation with helping spirits. In some cases, what is known as psychic surgery may be employed, but this will be discussed in a later chapter.

Ancient Healers

Looking back at various ancient civilisations, you find that both in ancient Egypt and ancient Greece, healers were commonplace. The ancient Egyptians have always been exceptionally well known as healers, and one of the most famous was Imhotep, who after his death became revered as the son of Ptah, Egyptian God of medicine and healing. In fact, many of these ancient healers in both Egypt and Greece became elevated to God status after their death because of their remarkable powers of healing.

Healing temples were set up in the name of Imhotep, and various statues erected. Hieroglyphics were normal upon such statues, and water was poured upon the statue to cleanse it, and the patient would subsequently drink from it. It was a normal thing to find many

sick people literally camping out within the temple to Imhotep at Memphis, and sometimes those too ill to travel sent friends or relatives to visit on their behalf. Healing was part of the normal pattern of events in temples in Egypt, and priests were healers, chosen to be so at birth in many cases, and having undergone strict training and study, emphasising from the outset that the human race is linked with the planet and that the mind is linked with the body. Most healing temples were exceptionally strict in their hygiene regulations, and it was also common for various herbal remedies to be suggested to those in need of treatment. The Egyptian knowledge of herbal remedies seems to have been quite extensive, and some minerals and vegetables were also used in healing treatments. In addition, various fragrances were used, and a full range of holistic treatments was common.

Outside the temple system, many villages would have had people within their midst capable of healing who would deal with varied problems, from broken bones to general illnesses and disease, but all these healers linked their healing to religious practices and belief systems, and many also had a wide knowledge of plants, herbs and minerals which could aid the healing process.

In Greek history, there are also many recorded examples of healers who successfully healed the ill. Around the same time as Imhotep was achieving fame in Egypt, Asclepius (also sometimes spelt Asklepios or Aesculapius) was receiving similar acclaim in Greece, and in much the same way as Imhotep, after Asclepius' death temples were built to him as a healing god. Most major cities had their temples to the gods of medicine. Worship of Asclepius spread to Rome after a plague in 293 BC and Homer refers to Asclepius as 'the incomparable physician'. Legend suggests that Asclepius, who was the son of Apollo and Coronis and born near Mount Pelion, taught healing and was given a knowledge of herbal medicine by Cheiron the centaur. He was reputed to be such a powerful healer that he was able to stop the flow of blood, and it is said that he cured Hercules, and later Galen (another famous healer) from a fatal disease. Galen later went on to practise healing for many years, and used dreams to diagnose illnesses. Stories tell that Asclepius often carried out surgery on patients who were then able to walk the

following day with no ill effects, and that sometimes he healed by touch alone. He also recommended to patients various dietary and exercise guidelines, as well as suggesting swimming, bathing and the taking of various medications, explaining that to obtain healing, it was also necessary for the patient to consider changing his or her way of life, a suggestion which also appears in the Bible.

Asclepius' death came about as a result of being hit by a thunderbolt, tradition suggests because he endeavoured to raise a dead man and thus angered Zeus. However, even after his death, reverence for him and his healing powers continued, probably for more than a thousand years, first as a demi-god and then as a full god.

The power of the mind was acknowledged by both the Greeks and the Egyptians, and it was also felt that the knowledge to heal could be given through dreams. As a result, people in both civilisations would sleep in the healing temples, hoping to receive a cure through their dream state.

Pythagorus and Hippocrates (after whom the Hippocratic oath which doctors take is named) both believed in healing through energy, and both men acknowledged the link between body and mind – holistic healing. In a similar fashion, most priests of ancient Greece believed that people had within themselves everything required to heal themselves, and that the only function they served was to help the person concerned discover this for themselves. As in ancient Egypt, most large cities had a healing temple or Asklepios, and there were annual festivals to honour the God of Medicine, and to ask for healing for all. Many people flocked to the healing temples in the large cities, both to ask for healing and to enjoy the wonderful surroundings in which the temples were set.

The use of water in healing treatments

In the Greek temples of healing especially, water played an important role in the healing process. Healing fountains were central features, and it was felt that one of the best self-cures was to drink from the healing fountains. In ancient Egypt, there was a similar belief in the power of water to heal, being charged by its passage through the earth.

This belief has, in many cases, continued into the present day. Most if not all healing temples were set within beautiful surroundings, as it was realised that a pleasant environment can also go some way to achieving a healing state. Likewise, music was an important part of the rituals within the healing temples, and Asclepius encouraged many people not only to write music but also to write poetry in order to reduce stress levels.

Temples at Kos, Pergamum and Epidaurus were considered to be the most beautiful places to visit, with their wonderful marble, ivory, gold and bronze statues, beautiful gardens and colonnades. In particular, it is said that Epidaurus was a spectacular sight, having been designed by Polyclitus, who was one of the most famous architects of the time.

In addition to its abilities to effect a cure from being ingested, water was used as part of a purification and cleansing process prior to healing, as it was felt to purify not only body but mind. At the temple at Pergamum, there was a stairway leading down to a tunnel which carried spring water in a channel formed out of the rocks. Patients were encouraged to make their way through this channel, which may have symbolised a passage to another world, while priests supervised, informing them of the healing powers they were receiving and telling them that they would soon be well.

Worldwide, water has always been considered to have special properties. In China around 100 AD, Chang Tao-ling, also known as the Celestial teacher, and the founder of magical Taoism, put forward the theory that illness was caused by sin, and asked patients to write down their sins and then bathe in a lake, promising never to sin again.

Water is indeed an important substance to us all, as without water we are unable to exist, and it is fair to say that many cultures, including the American Indians and Persians as well as the ancient Greeks and Egyptians, respected water and included it in healing. Lourdes, in France, is one of many religious places worldwide still visited today by those who are unwell, and there are spa towns where beneficial waters can be enjoyed. The word 'spa' comes from the Belgian resort of Spa, known for its medicinal waters. Bath in

England is a spa town, dating from 800 BC. The warmth and mineral qualities of the waters there are helpful in the treatment of all sorts of diseases. Other spa towns in the United Kingdom include Droitwich, Buxton, Cheltenham, Llandrindod Wells, Leamington, Malvern, Matlock, Tunbridge Wells, Strathpeffer, Woodhall and Harrogate.

Places with high energy levels

Certain places have a higher level of energy than others, a fact seized upon at an early stage in human development, which resulted in the erection of various structures, for example Stonehenge in England erected by the early Bronze Age people. These places are also the location for the siting of buildings given to healing and the treatment of illness. In China and the Far East, the siting of buildings for favourable effect is known as *feng shui,* and the Chinese consider feng shui before building houses, siting tombs and launching new ventures. 'Feng shui' means 'wind and water' and is the belief that mankind needs to live in harmony with the environment. Further details on feng shui can be obtained by reading *Feng Shui for beginners,* in this series.

In India and Japan, there are many healing temples and shrines, and the siting of such places is always considered of prime importance.

Healing in the Bible

There are many instances of healing recorded within the Bible, and I feel it is important to discuss these, as they are all examples, of spiritual healing, irrespective of religious belief. I would like to reiterate that a belief in God or in the Bible as the word of God is not vital to acceptance of spiritual healing as a form of treatment, but more important is the understanding of the way in which healing occurred in the past, so that we can compare it to the healing practices of our modern age. The Bible gives particular significance to details of healing, and healing, both physical and spiritual, is a major theme within its pages.

Many people think of healing of the sick as something which was demonstrated by Jesus, and that mention of spiritual healing starts only in the New Testament. In the Old Testament, however, there are many recorded instances of spiritual healing. In Job, we can read how Job, afflicted with various losses and illnesses, was cured of disease after praying. Praying for healing is still widely practised, and is known as charismatic healing from the Greek word *charis* meaning 'grace'. At many church meetings and religious groups, people meet to pray not only for healing for themselves but also for others, and in Catholic churches, this can often form part of a normal Sunday service. The Christian Scientists also encompass healing as an integral and, indeed, essential part of their religion.

Many believe that spiritual healing's links with Christianity and religion ceased with the demise of the twelve apostles, but many healings by St Justin and St Jerome are recorded, and indeed St Francis of Assisi is recorded as practising spiritual healing. During the Middle Ages, the Church actively encouraged the thought that healing could take place at the shrines of saints.

Healer Ambrose Worrall, whose work we have already discussed, is widely quoted as saying that all thoughts are prayers, and that prayers should be personal statements, rather than things learned parrot fashion and repeated. One of the most famous cases of charismatic healing is that of Sir Francis Chichester, the well-known, round-the-world yachtsman. He developed lung cancer when in his fifties, and spurning conventional treatment, relied on the prayers of his family and friends for a cure, in addition to receiving naturapathic treatment. He made a recovery, and three years later won the first solo transatlantic yacht race. We will discuss the power of affirmations and prayers in a later chapter, but suffice it to say at this point that it is generally accepted that prayer carried out in a group is far more powerful than prayer done by an individual, possibly due to a sychronising of energies of the group.

The Jewish sect known as the Essenes, who lived around the Dead Sea, regularly cast out demons, and spiritual healing formed a large part of their general beliefs, concerning both the healing of the body and of the spirit. It is thought that the Essenes were at their height

during the century before and the century after the birth of Christ, although there are records to show that they existed at least two centuries before the birth of Christ. Some scholars suggest that the belief system of the Essenes was the forerunner to Christianity, there being many similarities.

The Essenes' teaching encompassed what is known as the Sevenfold Peace; Peace with the Body is the first of these, and Peace with the Mind the second. As part of their training, the Essenes learned how disease is created by disharmony, and that healing comes about through regaining that harmony, both the body with itself and the body with its environment. Once achieved, it was felt that this harmony could heal all diseases. They learned about herbs and plants, about hydrotherapy and heliotherapy, and dietary guidelines which would help in healing treatments. They also learned how to breathe correctly and about the interrelationship between mind and body.

Records show that the sect probably numbered around 4,000, and much about their lifestyle has been learned through the discovery of the Dead Sea Scrolls, documents which are considered to be older than the earliest surviving Hebrew manuscripts of the Old Testament by around 1,000 years, and which are said to have belonged exclusively to the Essenes. Believing in sharing their possessions, piety, truthfulness and justice, these peace loving people rejected slavery, and there are various theories suggesting that John the Baptist was an Essene. Other scholars claim that, during his period of seclusion from the world, Jesus Christ studied with the Essenes, and point out that he frequently condemned the scribes, pharisees and sadduccees but not the Essenes, as would be the case if he himself had been one of their brotherhood. However, those believing Jesus to be the son of God will suggest that Jesus, being perfect and all-wise, would have had no need of outside study.

Within the Old Testament are details of the prophets Elijah and Elisha healing others. Elijah is credited with bringing back a widow's son from the dead through prayer in 1 Kings, and his successor, Elisha is recorded as raising people from the dead in 1 Kings and 2 Kings and also of healing Army Chief Naaman of leprosy. Other Old

Testament records of healing are to be found in Isaiah and Jeremiah, amongst other books.

However, most people will associate Jesus with spiritual healing, because of the amount of healing he undertook as part of his work, and irrespective of whether it is believed that Jesus was the Son of God, or just a wonderful example for future generations to follow, it is generally accepted that he was probably the greatest spiritual healer of all times.

During his ministry, which lasted only three-and-a-half years in total, Jesus healed the sick and restored the dead to life. Sometimes, as with spiritual healing in modern times, the healing was a gradual thing, but sometimes it was instantaneous, or miraculous. Just prior to the start of the twentieth century, Jean Martin Charcot, a French neurophysicologist, claimed that the form of healing which he, personally, practised was also 'miracle healing' and felt that most forms of disease, including cancer, could be cured. 'Commonly known in medical circles as miracle healing,' he said, 'in the majority of cases, it is merely a natural phenomenon which occurs throughout history at all times, at most levels of civilisation, and amongst most religions, however, they may otherwise differ.' Miracle cures have also been reported worldwide at sacred locations such as Lourdes in France.

Many people followed Jesus throughout his ministry in the hope that they would be healed or 'made whole'. Throughout his ministry, Jesus demonstrated unconditional love, and his healing of those who were ill is one of the many ways in which he showed his compassion for humanity.

It is important to recognise that Jesus had full faith and confidence that he would be able to heal, and made it clear that he himself was not the healer, but only a channel for the healing to be given. It should also be noted that it was not necessary for the ill to have faith in being cured (John 5), although most did have a strong faith.

More than forty accounts of Jesus' healing are recorded in the Bible. He healed the lame, maimed, blind and dumb, epileptic, paralytic, those who suffered from 'female problems', those with withered limbs, dropsy and various spiritual ailments, irrespective of whether

they had suffered from their ailment for many years or as a result of a recent event. Throughout the gospels of Matthew, Luke, Mark, John and Acts are details of Jesus' healing ministry, which he carried out every day, regardless of whether it was the Sabbath or not.

Jesus healed not only through touch, but through simple statements. Sometimes, the phrase 'Take up your bed and walk' was sufficient for a person to be healed, and at other times, even though there was a distance between Jesus and the person requiring healing, this healing was still given (Matthew 8). At other times, he actually touched those who were in need of healing, and in fact several people who simply touched Jesus or even his clothing were healed.

Jesus told his disciples that they, too, had the power to heal, and when they were sent out to minister to the world, they also healed the sick. One such incident is recorded in Acts 3, when Peter healed a beggar who had been lame from birth. Not only the twelve disciples had the power to heal, but so did other evangelisers, such as Paul. Also famous for healing, speaking in tongues and performing miracles after the death of Jesus were people known as the Montanists, who came from Phrygia, the Waldensians, Jansenists and the French Camisards.

Healing in the early Christian Church

In the early days of the Christian Church, there was much conflict between followers of Christ and followers of Asclepius, who was considered to have comparable ability. In fact, many people at that time considered that Jesus was merely a magician, having learned to develop his talents in Egypt. He was thought to be a man who worked with devils, and it is interesting to note that Ascelpius was viewed similarly. The conflict between the opposing factions continued for many years, and at one point it seemed that Asclepius had won, as more and more temples were erected to him. Eventually, however, Christianity succeeded in overthrowing these

sanctuaries, and in some cases transforming them into Christian shrines, so that the miracle cures could be seen to continue.

Various followers of Jesus were still healing, speaking in tongues and performing 'miracles', and we have to research only a small way into Christianity's history, to discover that a split soon occurred in the young Church between the elders and those who were seen to be carrying out healing, claiming to be from God. This group became known as the Gnostics. The word *gnosis* was understood to mean 'revelation', rather than 'knowledge' or 'understanding' as would be expected from a literal Greek translation, and Gnosticism is sometimes called 'the religion of knowledge' or 'the religion of insight, rather than being reliant upon faith.

It is not certain when the Gnostic group was formed. It may have been in existence for many years prior to the death of Jesus, tracing elements of Gnostic belief to Egyptian, Greek, Zoroastrian and Taoist philosophies. Alternatively, it may have formed in the early years of Christianity, and Gnostics were essentially Christians who inherited Jesus' esoteric teachings, sighting Simon Magus as the founder, the story of whom can be read in Acts. What is certain is that these people, considered to be heretics by the Church, had a wide following, and believed strongly in the power of self-knowledge, and thus self-healing. They were extremely prominant as a group in the first two centuries after the death of Christ, and various forms of modern-day therapy and Eastern philosophies would seem to have a common root with Gnosticism. The growth of the self-awareness and development faction in modern times owes much of its information to various Gnostic literature and writings. Many Christians in the early centuries also accepted Gnostic thoughts.

Essential to the philosophies of Gnosticism is the belief that to really understand anybody or anything, and to stand a chance of further development, either emotionally or spiritually, one first has to know, love and understand one's self. Belief in the Church and its leaders was felt to be a hindrance rather than a help in seeking the knowledge of God which its followers strove to attain. In addition, the Gnostics held a firm belief in the power of sound to motivate and calm, and various chants were felt to hold particular power.

Many people followed the Gnostic movement, and the Church was desperate to quell the apostasy which they felt was within their midst. Gnosticism attempted to amalgamate Christian beliefs with Oriental and Greek belief systems, and of special significance were the doctrines of Plato and Pythagoras. Some Gnostics, claiming to be Christian in ideology, questioned the suffering and death of Jesus, suggesting that God would not become involved with matter, confining his attentions purely to the spiritual.

One of the best-known Gnostic groups was the Alexandrian school of Valentius, which promoted many mystical thoughts, and Gnosticism was taught also in many Roman schools. As a result, many Gnostics were accused of being magicians, practising spells and consulting with demons, and it was left to the bishops and those high in rank within the Church to decide at which point Gnosticism departed from Christian teachings.

It is fair to say that during the early centuries of Christianity, considerable interest in magic and spells abounded, and due in the most part to the power of the Church, much of the literature and most of the groups were quashed. Gnosticism's power diminished, helped in no small part by Clement of Alexandria and his pupil Origen, who attempted to show that Socrates and Plato were forerunners of the Christian ethic.

By the late Middle Ages, the Gnostic movement was more or less wiped out, with the last persecution taking place in 1244 in France. Gnostic teachings were, however, kept alive by the Freemasons, Kabbalists and Rosicrucians in the main, and remnants of their teachings can still be found within the Mandeans in Iraq and Iran. The Rosicrucians, in particular, are still actively involved in spiritual healing, and also believe in taking 'self-help' measures to prevent disease and allow the body to heal itself. Students of the work of psychiatrist Carl Jung will be well aware of his interest in Gnosticism and healing through the power of the mind as well as through ancient belief systems.

By the fifteenth century, anyone claiming to perform miracles, speak in tongues or heal by the power of God or the Holy Spirit was believed to be a heretic, but many people continued to put forward their ideas. In

the sixteenth century for example, Paracelsus, a Swiss physician began to set out his philosophies, which included linking healing with a knowledge of astrology. Believing that God was human beings' main doctor, Paracelsus put forward the thought that the body was merely a home for the spirit, and that the two must be treated together for healing to take place, through a harmonising of elements. He felt that religion was the basis of medicine and that living in harmony with God and the universe should be the ultimate aim for all. As such, he felt that a healer should also be an astrologer, knowing all about harmony of the planets and their influences on the human mind.

Interest in spirituality and healing through self-knowledge has never completely died out, and spiritual healing continues to have a following throughout most of Europe and the West, especially in the work of the Druids, who worship in sacred oak forests, have a strong belief in the powers of Nature and practise herbal medicine, the erection of buildings on areas of land considered to have particular energy and healing potential, and so on. Such beliefs were actively discouraged by the early Christian Church, unless it could be linked with a particular saint, and it is well known how, even up to the early part of the twentieth century, groups of people who were considered heretics were persecuted, tracked down and killed, in order to maintain the position and power of the Church. In many cases, these people merely practised healing, but because they fell outside the Church's accepted position, they were classed as witches or in league with the devil, and dealt with accordingly. During the time of the Inquisition, many such people lost their lives.

MORE RECENT DEVELOPMENTS

As we have already learned, various groups and individuals continued to practise the art of spiritual healing, despite opposition from both the Church and political groups and governments, and many suffered ridicule and personal loss as a result. There are many recorded examples of those practising healing in its various forms who were ostracised by society, and even Anton Mesmer, whose work into

magnetism, energy fields and the power of the mind eventually led to studies being carried out into trancelike states and hypnotism, was branded a charlatan.

Fortunately, however, this was not always the case. Following on from the work of Mesmer was Charles Puyen, a Frenchman who moved to the United States in the early 1800s. For some time, he toured with a lady called Cynthia Gleason who, while under hypnosis, proved to be able to diagnose illness in people by slowly passing her hand over the patient's body, starting from the head and working downwards. Her diagnoses were startlingly accurate. Around the same time, in England, Daniel Dunglas Home was also exhibiting remarkable powers of healing, and at one time intended to study to become a doctor, but his own ill health prevented him from so doing.

There are many religious groups, not only the Spiritualist movement, who have continued to practise healing as part of their daily lives, and in the evangelical movement, and especially in what is called 'The Bible Belt' in the United States spiritual healing's presence is very much in evidence. The Pentecostal movement, for example, not only encourages speaking in tongues, but also the laying-on of hands for healing. Likewise, following the work and writing of Mary Baker Eddy, the Christian Scientist movement continues to practise spiritual healing of physical and emotional illnesses in an active way through knowledge of Jesus Christ and the Bible. Mary Baker Eddy felt strongly that there was a need to reinstate the lost element of healing within a Christian framework.

Within the twentieth century, there has been an increasing need for healing, and many famous healers have gained prominence. Dutch healer and worker for spirit Gerard Croiset, was just one such person, who treated over 100 patients a day at his healing clinic. Upon meeting his patients, Croiset said he knew immediately whether he could help or not, and often felt that diseases were connected to experiences. Croiset died in 1980, but his clinic has continued to operate under the direction of his son.

Another famous healer was Edgar Cayce, who while in a trancelike state gave out more than 14,000 readings aimed at helping the individual concerned, many containing detailed information on how

health and wellbeing could be improved by diet, potions and change in lifestyle. Despite being dismissed by the medical profession because of his lack of medical training, Cayce managed to diagnose illness accurately and prescribe remedies for anybody who asked, irrespective of whether they came for a personal appointment or asked by letter. All he needed was a name and address, and many of the remedies suggested by Cayce have subsequently been examined and proven to work in clinical studies. Cayce, who died in 1945, had the desire to build a hospital where the treatments recommended by him while in his trancelike state could be practised, but this venture failed. Cayce fervently believed that illness happened only when the body's energy systems were disturbed, and that healing could take place only through natural channels, through God, treating the whole body, rather than the symptoms. The formation of the Association for Research and Enlightenment has done much to ensure that the information given by Cayce is still accessible to all who seek it, and books produced by the ARE are well worth seeking out.

Olga and Ambrose Worrall, mentioned briefly earlier, devoted many years to their healing ministry, concentrating a great deal on the healing of children, as well as animals and birds. Other famous American healers and workers for spirit include Pat Rodegast and Eileen Garrett, whose work with American psychologist Lawrence LeShan is well detailed.

bealing camps and sanctuaries

Any discussion on spiritual healing in the twentieth century cannot fail to mention the extremely important work carried out by two British spiritual healers, Harry Edwards and Matthew Manning.

Harry Edwards, who died in 1976, set up a healing sanctuary in Surrey, which continues to operate and practise spiritual healing in an active way. During his lifetime, it is said that Mr Edwards received more than half a million letters every year, asking for

healing help. Likewise, Matthew Manning has a similar sanctuary, and travels the world aiming to help as many sick and ill people as he possibly can using the power of spiritual healing.

Famous within England for its healing work and spiritual teachings is the White Eagle Lodge in Liss, Hampshire. Here, a great deal of emphasis is placed on healing, which is carried out either in groups or individually, and also includes the laying-on of hands. A belief that the spirit requires healing before the body in order for lasting relief from symptoms and healing of illness to take place is paramount to the teachings given at the Lodge. Founded by Grace Cooke, a prominent worker for spirit and teacher of meditation, the organisation continues to expand and develop despite Grace Cooke's own death in 1979.

Within the United States, a well-known camp for spiritually minded people and those requiring healing is Lily Dale, in Chautauqua Country, New York. Each day during the summer months, visitors can go along to the healing temple, where as many as five healers help patients. All healers have recognised credentials in healing, which are available for inspection.

Away from any religious or spiritual organisation, many practioners of therapeutic touch work in a healing capacity for the benefit of patients. Developed by Dora van Gelder Kunz, a meditation teacher, and Dolores Krieger, a nurse, therapeutic touch teaches that universal energies, the life force, or what the eastern religious groups call *chi* is transmitted through touch, or holding hands over the body. Scientific tests have shown that the therapy does, in fact, increase the oxygen capacity of red blood cells, lowers high temperatures and has a calming effect on those treated. In Japan the therapy known as *Seiki-jutsu* works in a similar way, with the healer transferring energies through the crown of the head, down the spine and into the whole body.

As we have seen, spiritual healing is still an active force for helping human beings, and has been so from earliest times. In Chapter 3, we will concentrate on looking at the various philosophies connected with spiritual healing, at energy, breathing and relaxation.

3 ENERGY, LOVE AND SELF-HEALING

In Chapters 1 and 2, we learned a little about the history of spiritual healing and also about the Universal Power or energy it uses, and have seen how, throughout the ages, the utilising of this Universal Power had been able to help people with illness and disease.

In this chapter, we are going to take a far more detailed look at this energy, considering the Indian and Chinese ideas of Universal Power, which are gradually becoming accepted in the West. We will also learn how this power or energy around and within us all can be harnessed to activate self-healing, and take a look at the power of love, at breathing, relaxation and yoga to see how we can learn to heal ourselves, before we go on to heal other people.

Ch'ı or prana

Those readers familiar with yoga and relaxation may already be aware of the word *prana* meaning breath, life force or absolute energy, vitality and power, but may not be fully conversant with what it actually means. You may also recall that we mentioned pranic healing in an earlier chapter. Known not only to the yogis of India from ancient times, but also to the Egyptians, Hebrews, Tibetans, Chinese, Japanese and Greeks, this force was biblically given the name *Neshemet Ruach Hayim* meaning 'Breath of Spirit and Life', as mentioned in the book of Genesis, Chapter 2.

Prana (pronounced prahna) is essentially Sanskrit in origin, but as we now know, it has its parallels in other cultures – in China is it

ch'i, *shi* or *qi*, (pronounced 'chee') in Japan it is *ki* (pronounced 'kee'), in the Polynesian Islands it is *mana* and in Tibet it is *lung* (pronounced 'loong').

Prana is present in everything which lives. It is present not only in humans, but also in every plant, animal and micro-organism. The air we breathe, the sunshine, the earth, water, minerals, food – all these things contain prana. According to ancient Hindu teachings, prana is one of the most basic elements of the universe and is a divine power, being not breath but clearly revealed in breath. Prana is in and around us all – it flows through us and through all living things from the most complex of forms to the most basic, in a network of channels. It enters our bodies at birth and flows through us, undisturbed and balanced while we maintain good health. We need to have an abundant supply of prana to enjoy health and maintain the harmony we need, and we are given this at birth. We cannot add to the amount of prana we have, but we can reduce it dramatically by our lifestyle, our mental attitude and diet, in addition to other outside factors. Once the balance or harmony is disturbed, our prana is also disturbed, and ill health or disease results.

You will remember, right at the start of this book, how I described a situation where someone is tense, and in an attempt to dissipate the anger, you remain calm and detached, maybe focusing on a colour as well, and see how you can restore calm to both them and the situation. It is well known how our mental attitudes can and do affect us, but all we are really doing is trying to keep our own harmony and balance – maintaining our prana – and transfer some of this in a positive way to the other party. You only have to see how stress can bring about headaches, digestive problems and the like to see how our life force can be influenced. Prana, being the life force, or universal energy, also has the power to heal, and once we find ourselves able to link into its power, we can bring about our own self-healing, as well as the healing of others.

We have already established that the body can be healthy only when everything, including prana or ch'i, is in harmony. That also includes the mind and the environment, and we have seen through our researches into history how most civilisations have known and come to accept this. We have also discussed how certain areas of

the world have been thought to contain more power than others. Hindus tend to believe that prana is more concentrated at the top of mountains and near running water.

To the Chinese, this balancing act is well expressed in terms of yin and yang. Yin is darkness, while yang is light. Yang is active, masculine and powerful, while yin is feminine, passive and gentle. Yang controls heaven and yin controls Earth, and these polarities, of which the whole universe is composed, are fundamental to Chinese philosophy. The organs of the body and their meridians (see below) are further divided into yin and yang, When we are upset, angry or stressed we have an excess of yang and yin, and consequently the balance of our prana is disrupted. We need to be like a balanced scale, with both sides equal, in order to operate effectively and be well.

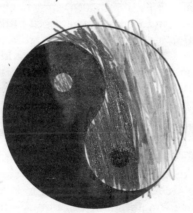

Meridians

The Chinese believe that the Universal Power of ch'i flows through the body in twelve main channels, or meridians, all of which relate to specific organs of the body or bodily functions. This Universal Power flows in a specific direction and fluctuates with the seasons and the time of day. Therapies such as acupuncture, auricular therapy, moxibustion, acupressure, polarity balancing and reflexology, for example, seek to trace and use these meridians, and ultimately

to relieve blockages in the ch'i or prana, to dissipate the imbalances which can be caused by physical, emotional or environmental factors, and restore harmony to the body.

Chinese history shows the earliest record of ch'i being linked to health and healing comes from the Han Dynasty (206BC–220AD). In a book known as *The Yellow Emperor's Classic of Internal Medicine*, thirty-two forms of ch'i are described, and meridians discussed.

Even though the existence of meridians has been accepted by many for years, they have been the subject of scientific tests. Tests have taken place to confirm the existence of meridians, and they can now be plotted electrically with temperature-sensitive liquid crystal. Some psychics and clairvoyants also claim to be able to see meridians with the naked eye.

During scientific tests, a heat stimulus is applied to the acupuncture points on each meridian, the skin having been coated with temperature-sensitive liquid crystal. These tests have shown that as the heat passes through the meridian, the colour of the liquid crystal changes along the meridian line. Further tests in Japan, attempting to link the meridians with connective tissues which are rich in water, have suggested that there may be a connection between the meridian lines and the cycles of the moon and sea temperatures. Further research into meridians will, no doubt, continue.

Becoming sensitive to the Universal Power

Ch'i or prana is a form of electrical energy – you may find it helpful to think of the meridians as a sort of electric grid inside the body, through which this universal energy runs.

So we all have Universal Power within us, and we can also tap into it, but before we learn how to feel it in ourselves, let's take an example of how we already feel this universal force, but may not be aware of it.

During the course of a day, we invariably come into contact with other people. As John Donne said in the seventeenth century, 'No man is an island'. Since Donne's time, the human race has developed, and things which he could in no way imagine are now commonplace in our streets. Unfortunately, with advancement in technology and understanding came pollution, and by this I am referring not only to toxic fall-out from various nuclear tests or to the pollution from cars and other transport, but to everyday pollution from equipment which is now a feature of our homes and working lives.

During the course of our day, we meet not only other people, but also come into contact with electrical equipment – telephones, computers, etc., all of which emit energy. When we return from a day at work, we may have a wash, shower or bath, change our clothes and then relax. Is it just to clean ourselves up, or is it perhaps for some more fundamental reason, buried deep within our subconscious?

I would suggest that what we are doing when we wash and then change is really ridding ourselves of other people's energies and negative energies from our modern age, which have touched us during the day.

Let's imagine a typical scene for most working people. You leave home and travel to work. If you travel on a bus, tube or train, you will come into close contact with other people. Even if you drive to work, you will come into contact with others when you park your car, or wait at traffic lights, for example. When you arrive at work, there are other people around, and you are hardly likely to get through the day without actually touching someone else, either purposely or accidentally. In your lunch break, you go to the canteen or into a shop to buy something to eat, or you may go shopping or to pay some bills or go for a drink or meal with colleagues in a pub or restaurant. Again, you will come into physical contact with other people. You may even bump into people as they jostle to get past you. You may also notice how, when in a queue, some people tend to stand really close to you, invading your space; sometimes this may be a pleasant feeling, whereas some people may irritate you by standing so close, through no fault of their own. You

have already become sensitive to the energies of others. Some people are so sensitive to these energies that they can also pick up on emotional problems – they feel that there's 'something in the air'. They are sensitive to other people's energies.

Some of us may work with computers, or live near to electric power lines. Some of us may also work with microwave cookers or actively use telephones. Nearly all of us will have a television. All these things contain energy, and pollutive energy at that. It is now a well-recorded fact that those of us who live near electricity pylons will have a greater than average incidence of illness, both mental and physical. Likewise, new studies suggest that the use of computers, microwaves and even mobile telephones can increase the risk of illness or disease. I work with computers a great deal, and find after a few hours' working that I get a headache and have to stop. I know that I could personally never work in an office with computers all day without being ill.

Basically, the energy within and around us is being distorted and disturbed by artificial energy, and one of the easiest ways for us to clear ourselves of this on a daily basis is to wash it away.

We have already mentioned the healing powers of water, but maybe did not appreciate that it still heals us today, even if we don't actively seek out spa towns. Irrespective of what the water companies may have done to improve our water supplies or not as the case may be, water is still essentially a natural substance and a great conductor of electricity at that, and by using that natural substance, with its own natural energy, we are going a small way to recreating the harmony we need in our own energy field. We are also helping ourselves to relax, especially if we allow ourselves time for a long bath, with perhaps some gentle music and some pleasant smelling oils.

In a similar way, we wash our clothes, even though they may not actually be dirty, and we may use agents which create a nice smell on them.

We change our clothes to change not only our appearance but the way we feel. Few of us will wear chic clothing to lie around the house in. We 'dress up' or 'dress down' to suit the occasion and our

moods, and most of us will have noticed how various colours can and do affect us. We will be taking a deeper look at the power of colour in a subsequent chapter.

When we take off our working clothes and put on something more comfortable, not only are we mentally preparing ourselves for a different set of circumstances, but we are also ridding ourselves of the energies which those clothes have picked up during the course of the day.

So, we are perhaps already aware of Universal Power but perhaps hadn't considered it as a force before. Having established and identified its existence, though, how can we utilise it to positive effect for healing?

I have already explained that it us necessary for us to be well before we can even contemplate trying to carry out healing on other people, even absent healing or distance healing.

Spiritual healing taps into the universal energy rather than the energy systems within each one of us. Tapping into our own energy systems will merely deplete our supplies, which will then mean any healing is reduced in its efficacy and we will end up feeling run down. However, we do need to see how to generate more energy for ourselves, and so we will try a couple of really simple exercises which you can practise at any time and anywhere. These will help you to become more sensitive to both your own energy and that of other people. In later chapters, we will try other exercises which will help us actually to begin healing.

EXERCISES IN AWARENESS

During the course of these exercises, you should start to become aware of the passage of the ch'i energy. You may feel a sort of tingling sensation, a magnetic pull or a heat.

EXERCISE ONE

When we are cold, we often rub our hands together. We feel that it helps us to become warmer by stimulating our circulation. Let's

pretend that our hands are two sticks. When you rub two sticks together, you get a spark, and from that spark you can create fire. What happens when we rub our hands together is that we really create an energy, a spark. We can then use this energy to aid relaxation and help with the healing process.

Try rubbing your hands together, then place your hands immediately in front of your face and nose, close your eyes, and breathe in the heat and ch'i energy produced. You are helping to take this energy into your body, through your lungs and into your bloodstream. Take deep breaths, as this will help with overall relaxation. You may also wish to try keeping your eyes open and, without focusing directly on to your hands, allow the energy to be absorbed through your eyes. I have found this particularly useful when suffering from eyestrain or headaches. What we are doing is using the ch'i energy to revitalise us.

Exercise two

This exercise will help you to become sensitive to ch'i. Stand or sit in a relaxed position, with head lifted and shoulders back and down, and place your hands in front of you at chest level with palms facing but not touching. Take your hands a little further apart, and then bring them back together and concentrate on the feelings you will encounter between your hands. You can try doing this by taking your hands really quite wide, even as wide as shoulder distance apart, or turning the hands above or below one another, but all the movements should be slowly executed. Try this out in a calm environment, somewhere warm and peaceful but not hot.

You may also want to try this latter exercise with another person. Sit facing each other, and put your hands close to those of your partner, then move them away. If you try this exercise with various partners you will begin to realise how different people's ch'i varies. I have found that people who are in a healing profession, or those who are naturally gifted spiritual healers will have really powerful energies, and you can sometimes feel this to be so intense that you feel pushed away by the very force and power of it all. Conversely, those who are unwell or who are just feeling below par will have less energy. You may also discover how sometimes there seems more

energy in one side of the body than another, and it is generally accepted that we all have more ch'i on one side than another, as a result of body posture, blockages, illness or injury.

LOOKING AT LOVE

When someone says the word 'love', what immediately comes into your mind? Perhaps you think of family or friends, and the warmth of affection you feel towards them. Maybe you think about romance or even about sex, or the state of 'being in love'.

Love is all of these things, and a lot more besides. According to the dictionary, love is warm affection, benevolence, charity, sexual passion and delight; but is that all? I prefer to think of love as an unconditional thing, a great force and power, which can be given, not only to other people, but also to ourselves. I also like to think of love as a healing power, something which keeps us in harmony both with ourselves and with others, not just with 'God' as a power or as a concept, as I am well aware that not everyone will have a belief in God. However, if you substitute 'Universal Power', for the word 'God' and consider this as love, you will appreciate that the power we are discussing is in fact love – an extremely powerful thing.

Let's consider love as a force which we have at our disposal, should we care to use if for the good of others and for ourselves. Now let's look at the other side of the coin. If you are angry or tense, you are not showing love. Not only may you be showing a lot of hostility to others, but you are also not showing love to yourself. By creating this tension within yourself, by denying yourself the power of love, you are further creating blockages in your ch'i or energy systems. You may perhaps feel knots in you stomach. Your muscles will be tense, and basically you will not be at harmony with yourself.

I believe that to learn about healing also means that we have to learn about love, for healing is love. If we sincerely want to heal others, we have to desire to, deep down. We have to have a genuine love of that other person and really want to see them well.

A long time ago, I came to realise that we were all created out of love, and by that I don't mean the act of lovemaking. We were created by a force which was the epitome of love. I fully appreciate that those amongst us who disbelieve in an ultimate power may find this difficult to accept. However, I believe that we should all love each other, unconditionally, and by so doing, we will be taking a huge step in healing ourselves, other people, and ultimately the planet.

In any relationship, whether it is a close, intimate relationship or something more of an acquaintanceship, I try to demand nothing of others, neither do I expect anything in return. I believe in trying to be totally altruistic, living and behaving for the good of others, as well as for my own personal inner peace. That doesn't mean that I would allow other people to ride roughshod over me and my emotions. That would be foolish to the extreme, and there are times when I certainly take a firm stand. We all have to stand up and be counted, and at many occasions in our lifetimes, we will come across those who seek to knock us down. Learn to say 'No' occasionally, and learn to forgive, even if you don't forget, and you are going some way towards accepting the power of unconditional love. To forgive isn't to condone or minimise the wrongs that others have committed but involves letting go of resentment and bringing in the power of love.

As a race, we are all one, irrespective of the colour of our skin, our backgrounds, our ethics, morals – whatever. If we really wish to heal other people, as well as heal ourselves, we cannot allow any bigotry, hatred or prejudice to influence us, either in thought or action.

This can be really hard. There are times I feel anger, although not hatred, towards other people. However, what does that achieve? It makes me tense, thus blocking my flow of ch'i. It creates a tension in the room with the other people. That then disturbs the environment's own ch'i. What is the result of all this? I feel unwell. I learned a long time ago that hatred is a powerful thing, whereas dislike for a person or a situation is a slightly lesser thing. I, therefore, prefer to subdue thoughts of hatred, replacing these with a feeling of dislike, which I can more easily control. If I work on this, I can turn

this into a feeling of unconditional love, even if I still don't like the situation. In the Bible, even Jesus, considered to be the ultimate healer, showed anger when he threw the money changers out of the temple. He wasn't a soft touch, and neither should we be.

Sometimes the body really needs to release tension through action, either verbal or physical, and it is not a good idea permanently to turn anger inwards. There are those who firmly believe, for example, that there are various psychological links between anger and cancer, siting those who suffer with cancer as being generally nice people who find difficulty showing their emotions, anger being one of these. Maybe it was my own cancer in 1987 which brought me to the realisation that I should be more open with my emotions. I am not really sure when the 'transformation' began, but it is a gradual process which evolves over a period of years, and nobody should think that it will happen overnight, in much the same way as it would be foolish to think that one session of spiritual healing will provide a cure, if a cure can be achieved.

Reconsidering breathing and relaxation

Earlier on in this chapter, we mentioned 'The Breath of Life', and we really need to take a closer look at this if we are to consider self-healing.

Breathing is something we all take for granted. We all do it, subconsciously. Some of us will take deeper breaths than others, some will breathe more quickly than others, but we all breathe. How we breathe has a distinct link with how we are feeling. When we are asleep, our breathing is generally deeper and slower than when we are awake. If we are tense or scared, our breathing rate increases. Likewise, if we are exercising or carrying out a physical action, quite often our rate of breathing will increase. We will discuss lifestyle, including exercise in a subsequent chapter, but for the moment, let's just say that it is our breathing that shows that we are alive. However,

most of us really have no idea how to breathe properly, how to get the most from breathing, and we need to see how to improve our own breathing. We also need to see how this links into the state of relaxation and reduction of stress and tension which we all need.

There are many good books explaining about meditation, and we do not have sufficient space here to discuss meditation in any great detail, neither are we able to discuss yoga, which is a really beneficial form of relaxation through controlled, gentle exercise. However, we can discuss relaxation and how breath control can aid in the relaxation process.

Everybody is capable of relaxing properly, and breathing deeply and slowly. Some people, feeling that they will never be able to achieve this by themselves, seek out therapists to help them, or buy relaxation tapes. However, everyone can relax, given the time and the inclination. First you have to be aware of your body, your mental and emotional state, and also be aware that your body needs to relax, just as your mind needs to blank off from time to time.

Relaxation isn't just sitting down in a chair by the television. Relaxation is letting go of tensions and stresses, or what psychologists would call the 'fight or flight' reaction. When we are relaxed, our brainwave activities change, and this can be measured using an EEG machine.

In normal day-to-day activities, we are in a state of beta – being ready and prepared for most circumstances. When we are relaxed, we slow our brainwaves down to an alpha state. When we are half asleep, these brainwaves change to a theta state, and when we are in a deep sleep, we are in a delta state. What we are trying to achieve for a state of wellbeing is an alpha state.

As you can see from this quick explanation, we really do know, somewhere deep down, how to change our brainwaves, and thus change our breathing at the same time, but we generally don't actively seek to do so during our day.

BREATHING EXERCISE

One of the best ways to learn how to breathe correctly, is to take time

out to simulate sleep. I am not suggesting that you take a nap, because this is a totally different thing. Take yourself off to somewhere quiet, as we discussed in Chapter 1, and either sit down in a comfortable chair, or lie down. Don't cross your arms or legs – not only does this adversely affect your circulation, but it also hinders the path of the ch'i energies.

Start to concentrate your thoughts on your breathing, rather than on an object as we did before. Try to take deeper breaths, and breathe more slowly. I normally try to breathe in to a ten count, and then breathe out to another ten count, to avoid hyperventilation. In early stages of practising this new concept, try not to take more than five or six breaths. You may find it makes you slightly light-headed, because you really aren't used to such a huge input of oxygen. After a period of time, you will be able to extend the amount of deep breathing you can do.

Try to visualise yourself somewhere warm – you can even imagine yourself on a warm beach somewhere, if you like! Wherever you might picture yourself, remember that you are safe, warm and well. Just let yourself go into this fantasy place for a while. As you do so, you will become aware of your body becoming more relaxed, and you will also notice that your breathing slows down.

Relaxing your body

However, your body and its muscles may not be relaxed enough. It is, therefore, necessary to progressively relax your body. It is better to start off from the feet and work upwards.

Think about one of your feet. Think of its size, shape, texture, feel; think about how it is resting on the floor or, if you are lying down, on the mattress. Feel the tension in your foot, in your toes, in your ankle, and relax it. You may want to screw up your toes, and then relax them to achieve this. Now compare the relaxed foot with the other foot, and use the same method on the unrelaxed foot.

Using a similar procedure, work your way mentally from your feet to your legs, to your bottom and lower body areas, to the lumbar area of your lower back (a problem area for many), upwards through the

spine, into the shoulders. All this takes time, and you must be prepared to spend that time to achieve a properly relaxed state.

Carry on then working on relaxing your arms, hands and fingers. You will start to feel so relaxed that you may be unable to move, and think that your body doesn't belong to you. Don't even try to move. This state is what we have set out to achieve.

The last three areas to relax should always be the face, chest and the stomach, which for most of us is the most tense part of the body. Take a few really deep breaths. Let you facial muscles relax, let your stomach relax and breathe as deeply as you possibly can.

If you can stay in this supremely relaxed state for a while, that's great. Try to allow yourself at least twenty minutes, but if that isn't possible, try to stay there for ten minutes. Ideally, you should endeavour to carry out this exercise on a daily basis, probably at the end of the day, but some people, believing that they achieve more throughout the day from starting off relaxed, will do this exercise first thing in the morning.

Relaxing during the day

There are many other exercises you can practise to help with self-healing and stress reduction. If you find yourself feeling tense during the course of the day, especially in the shoulder area, take a deep breath in through your nose, bring your shoulders up to your ears, squeeze hard, and then let your shoulders fall, breathing out at the same time through your mouth. Doing this a few times will soon help you to lower your stress levels and become more focused.

If you have the time, do try to do some walking during the day. We will discuss lifestyle and exercise later, but it is important to realise that changing our environment to something more natural can and does help with self-healing. Just 'stretching your legs' with a short walk can do wonders for your mental and physical state.

I suggest that you take time out before starting on the next chapter to practise some of these exercises. In Chapter 4, we are going to take a more detailed look at our body's energy centres, our chakras and our aura, as well as discussing various aids we can employ in healing.

4

LOOKING AT AURAS AND CHAKRA CENTRES

*A*s part of learning about healing ourselves and others, we have been taking a detailed look at the Universal Power, what it is, how the body responds to it, and how it runs through the body in channels. In this chapter, we are going to take this a step further and look at how the body's energy is reflected by what is known as its aura, how this can be seen, and how it reflects our state of health, both physically and mentally. Also sometimes known as the Od, Odyle or Ordic force, we need to fully understand the aura if we are to learn to heal successfully, as most spiritual healers, as well as many other complementary therapists, will work with the aura. We also need to prove to ourselves that auras do exist and look at scientific tests aimed to establish that. We will also take a look at the energy centres within the body, known as the chakra centres, and how various forms of diagnostic and healing techniques can be used in conjunction with these centres and with the aura. Both auras and chakras are connected to colour, so we will also consider this.

AURAS

We already know that the human body has energy running through it, which we have likened to electricity. We have also seen how this electricity is present around us in the environment, and indeed in the universe as a whole. This energy radiates from the body. All living things, whether plants, animals or human beings give off an energy, and this is called the aura. This aura is basically what we

were discussing in Chapter 3, when we were looking at picking up other people's energies.

Since ancient times, people have believed in the existence of the aura, and it appears in the writings and art of many ancient cultures and civilisations, including, not surprisingly, those of Egypt, Greece, Rome and India. The aura has also became the subject of many superstitions, and even today, there are some Chinese who believe the aura to be the devil. Another race of people believed that the aura around the head protected them from death, so wore tall hats to contain it.

Various cultures over the years sought to record the aura of people in artwork, and many aboriginal rock paintings in Australia show auras around people. There are those who will also point to Renaissance drawings of biblical characters who are depicted with a halo around the head, suggesting that this is really showing an aura.

Despite the fact that various therapies using the universal energies have become more and more accepted, the aura has to many remained something of a grey area, regardless of the writing of respected men such as Paracelsus, Emanuel Swedenborg and Mesmer.

There have always been those who actively believe that the body has an aura, but until the arrival of the twentieth century, much of this was based on theory or statements made by psychics or sensitive healers, rather than anything more tangible. Even now, with various scientific tests, there are those who will denounce the existence of the aura. While most will agree that the body does have its own magnetic field, known as the biofield, those people who claim to be able to see the aura as a light or as a series of colours with the naked eye tend to be those who are practising clairvoyants or psychics.

TESTING THE PRESENCE OF THE AURA

Since the mid-nineteenth century, many respected scientists have sought to prove the existence of the aura. Tests carried out in 1845

by Reichenbach, a German chemist, during work with clairvoyants sitting in a darkened room, suggested that colours emanated from various objects. However, science still looked to prove or disprove such theories which had existed since ancient times. As we are now aware, scientific tests were carried out to show the body's energy meridians, and it will, therefore, come as no surprise to learn that tests have been done over the years to try to record or photograph the aura.

For many years, from the 1870s until the early part of the twentieth century, Dr Walter Kilner, a physician in charge of electrotherapy at a London hospital, worked actively to prove the existence of the aura and in 1911 published a book called *The Human Aura*. This was viewed sceptically by many but, undaunted he continued with his experiments, and just prior to the First World War discovered that something surrounding patients' bodies could be seen if viewed through a glass screen coated with dicyanin, which made ultraviolet light visible. He saw this energy extend six inches around the whole body of patients, and discovered that the auras of males and females differed – adult females having a more refined appearance.

Kilner also noticed how these rays differed between those who were in good health and those who were not, and by the end of the First World War, he had discovered how illness affects the aura, either in part or in whole, and how those people who are ill can and do draw from the auras of those around them who are healthy. In 1920, Kilner revised his earlier book, and due to the experiments which had been carried out in the interim period, the book this time was treated with less scepticism. His work was continued by biologist Oscar Bagnall, who designed a pair of goggles with lenses filled with dicyanin, leading to a clearer definition of the aura. Many people have subsequently learned to see the aura through the goggles and have even gone on to learn how to see auras without such equipment.

Around the same time as Kilner was investigating auras, work to photograph them began. Known as 'electrography', research was first published by a Czechoslovakian called Navratil during the early 1900s. Research continued, and in 1939, two more Czechoslovakians, Prat and Schlemmer, published photographs of what they felt was the aura around leaves. Likewise in 1939, a Russian engineer from Krasnodar, called Semyon Kirlian and his wife Valentine, a biologist,

attempted to record the human aura on film, and what is now known as Kirlian photography was discovered. This type of high-voltage photography, which Kirlian and his wife worked on for the next forty years, shows up auras around life forms (not only around humans) in colours and shapes. Early Kirlian photographs were in black and white, but eventually, following refinement of the equipment used, colour photographs became possible.

During an accident whilst repairing laboratory equipment, Kirlian received an electric shock, when a spark was emitted from the machine in question. Wondering whether this could be recorded on film, he put a sheet of light-sensitive paper between another electric spark and his own hand. He took a photograph, which when developed showed his fingers surrounded by light. He also discovered when seeking to show other scientists of his work at a time when he was in the early stages of a cold, that the aura around his hand showed up as only a faint blur, while that of his wife, who at the time was in good health, remained clear and bright.

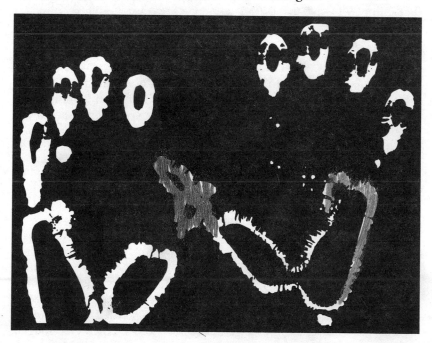

Since that time, various scientists have investigated Kirlian photography, notably Romanian Dr Ion Dumitrescu and American therapist James Knightlinger. Many have used Kirlian photography as a diagnostic tool, linking its useage with knowledge of chakra centres of which we will learn more later, although to many, the whole issue of Kirlian photography remains controversial, suggesting that all the photographs show is energy which can be produced only under certain conditions. However, it is well known that the Russians have continued to use Kirlian photography, especially in sports training as a means of assessing an athlete's fitness level and health, because the aura will often show up problems in a person's mental or physical state before physical symptoms appear.

Little was known outside the Communist block about the research taking place into auras until the early 1960s, when it was publicised widely that various Soviet scientists, including biophysicist Viktor Adamenko, had learned that that the brightest points of the aura were situated around the Chinese acupuncture points. This had, in fact, already been established to some degree by a collaboration between Kirlian and Leningrad surgeon Mikhaila Gaikin, who actually constructed an electronic locator for the acupuncture points.

Further tests into auras have and will continue, and current researchers have come to see how, when part of a leaf has been cut from a plant, its aura can still be recorded on film after its removal from the main body of the plant. This type of experiment, known as 'phantom leaf', is sometimes linked to the feelings amputees have that their missing limb is still part of their body.

According to Dr Kilner, auras can be divided into three main layers. These three layers are of differing thickness. The first layer, or outer aura, is of various sizes up to one foot in depth, while the second or emotional layer is fairly constant in size (normally about three inches) and density. The third, spiritual or etheric layer, is narrow (its thickness perhaps dependent upon the spirituality or not of the person concerned), and sometimes it is seen actually to merge with the second layer. Current thought is that the aura can extend from a few inches up to an arm's length or more away from the body, and that it will be more concentrated around the head area. As we have already discussed, it can change in colour and brilliance with the

onset of illness or injury, and is normally composed of seven colours (see pages 57–59).

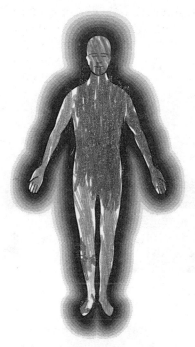

LEARNING TO SEE THE AURA

It is important for anybody who wishes to carry out healing to be familiar with the aura and how it shows up problems in health, so we must now learn how to see the aura for ourselves, without the aid of goggles or other equipment. There are various tests we can do, both by ourselves and with other people, and we will discuss several alternatives so that you have a choice and can make up your own mind which you prefer.

Disease first appears in the outer layers of the aura, and symptoms of the illness occur at a later stage. If we are able to train ourselves to see the aura, we can also attempt to 'nip a problem in the bud'. However, it is worthwhile remembering that it takes time and practice to be

able to achieve this. Don't be too upset or disappointed if you don't see results first time. You might not even see colours, but some sort of light, so don't be too hard on yourself, and keep practising.

EXERCISES TO SEE THE AURA

EXERCISE ONE

Find somewhere comfortable, warm and private, away from any distractions. You will also need a mirror. The room should have plain walls if possible, so that you are not bothered by reflections of things which would allow your mind to wander. Using the relaxation and breathing techniques we have already discussed, and which by now you should find quite easy, sit or stand directly in front of the mirror, looking at the centre of your forehead. Don't stare or try too hard, but just look gently. After a short period of time, you should see colours around your head. As these become apparent, allow your gaze to lower to the chin and neck area, and you should also then start to see the aura around your neck and shoulders. As you then bring your focus back to the forehead area, your colours should be quite visible, as a band around your body, and you may be able to make out certain shades.

EXERCISE TWO

Another way of learning to see the aura involves another person, preferably someone who is amenable to the experiment! Opinions differ as to whether it is best to get your friend to stand in front of a light or even white background, or a dark or black background. I will leave it for you to make your own choice here. Having got your friend in position, focus your eyes on the person's forehead (some people suggest focusing on the nose), and you should gradually notice colours round the face, and then around the whole body.

What do the colours mean?

There are various interpretations about what auric colours actually mean, and I would suggest that you form your own conclusions, based on experience and practice. However, as a starting point, here are some generally accepted guidelines. Some people suggest that there are only seven principal colours of the aura, but I have broadened this out to make it easier to understand.

White

Very rare to see this, as it is only spiritually advanced people who have white auras, and I doubt if anybody will actually get to see a white aura. Remember, when you start to try to develop the ability to see auras, you may see a sort of white cloud – this isn't a white aura.

Black

Not a good thing to see, representative of someone who is revengeful, malicious or even evil.

Grey

Depression, fear, lack of self-esteem, etc. are all shown by a grey aura. People with grey in their aura are normally people who are negative in character.

Brown

Materialistic, earthy person, who is keen to get ahead and will possibly be greedy and power conscious.

Blue

Lots of different shades here for what is generally accepted as a highly spiritual colour. Very spiritual people have a violet tint to their blue aura or have a dark blue aura, while those who are possibly less advanced will have a lighter blue. Almost any kind of blue in an aura is a good sign.

INDIGO OR VIOLET

This indicates someone on a spiritual quest or search, with high moral values. You may note how these colours will change and alter with experiences or understanding. Generally speaking, those who have a purple aura will be quite overbearing, and heart or stomach difficulties are normally associated with those with indigo, violet or purple in their aura, although to some healers, those with indigo in their auras are generally calm individuals, unless the colour seems unbalanced, in which case the opposite applies.

GREEN

Again lots of different types of greens, but generally green is a sign of someone who is adaptable and caring. Light green generally indicates someone who is kind, while a darker green shows someone who is tactful and diplomatic. Lots of people who work in the health industry will have these types of green or even emerald green in their aura. Really washed-out greens indicate someone who is insincere, deceitful or untrustworthy. Muddy greens are normally people who suffer from envy and jealousy. On a personal note, I always know when I am about to be unwell, because, when I close my eyes, I always see lime green.

YELLOW

Wisdom, friendliness, happiness and intellect are shown by yellow in the aura, and those who are permanently seeking knowledge and know how to look after themselves have quite vivid yellow auras. Most would agree that egg yolk-coloured auras are a rarity, while lemon colours are far more common, often indicative of indecisiveness.

ORANGE

Depending on the shade, people with a little orange in their auras are generally thoughtful people (unless there's a lot of brown in there, too) and it is fair to say that they also often have kidney problems. Those with a great deal of orange in their auras are strong personalities with high ambitious desires, linked perhaps with fears of failure.

Red

Feelings, energy and emotions are shown by red auras, the stronger the passion, the brighter the red. Crimson auras show love, while duller crimson shows passion, both emotional and physical. One of the nicest auras is the rose-pink hue, which shows unconditional love – a love totally lacking in selfishness, not to be confused with coral which shows immaturity. At the other end of the scale, a deep, dull red is the red of anger and rage, and someone possibly quite domineering and suffering from stress, while a lighter red can indicate tension and stress.

How the aura will look

It would be unwise to assume that the colours about which we have learned will be seen as definite bands around the body, clear in form and shape. This isn't the case, as we must appreciate that the aura and its colours will depend a great deal not only upon the state of physical health, but on the state of mind of the person concerned.

Most healers will agree that someone with clearly defined bands of auric colour is someone who is unbending and hard, both on themselves and on others. Someone, on the other hand, with an aura of colours which merge into each other is likely to be a person who can be influenced by other people. Sometimes the aura will seem just like a lot of dull colours, normally indicating either ill health or someone who is really in need of a complete break. At other times, dark patches may be seen in the aura, and various healers believe that this indicates the presence of disease in that particular area.

Often, an aura will be seen as bands with sparks coming from each band, and it is really up to the individual, with practice and experience, to learn for him or herself what this means.

Using the aura in healing

We will discuss this in greater detail in a later chapter, but for now, let's just appreciate that when carrying out healing, most trained complementary therapists, including those who practise spiritual

healing and therapeutic touch, will run their hands around the body, looking to see signs of illness or disharmony in the aura, and then concentrate their healing on the specific area or areas requiring attention. Some healers will actually touch the body part concerned, so that the healing energy can flow through the healer's hands to the patient, while others will concentrate on healing the aura and the patient will not be touched at all.

Learning how to maintain a healthy aura

We need to keep ourselves healthy. As part and parcel of this need, we also need to maintain and build a healthy aura if we possibly can. We will be discussing in a later chapter how diet, exercise and lifestyle alterations can help towards this end, but we should realise from what we have learned to date that a proper diet, adequate sleep, reduction in stress and correct mental attitude will help us, and our auras, to be healthy. Remember what we have learned about the power of love and about universal energies, and apply the knowledge we have learned. We should also realise the importance of proper breathing, and how relaxation, as well as adequate physical exercise, is an important component of a healthy and strong body and aura.

Chakra centres

Readers who are familiar with yoga may already be fully conversant with the term *chakra*, from the Hindu meaning 'wheel', as chakras are said to be shaped like the spokes of a cartwheel and rotate at various speeds for the whole of our lifetime. As the chakras spin, they radiate out the Universal Power to the glands to which they correspond, and also out into the aura. If you are interested in finding out more about chakras in detail, read *Chakras for beginners* in this series.

Chakras are discussed in many Hindu and Buddhist writings, but as yet there is no accepted scientific evidence that they actually exist,

although some doctors will now acknowledge their existence, along with the acceptance of the energy meridians within the body.

Hiroshi Motoyama has been working for some time in Japan to prove the existence of the chakra centres by working actively with those who have studied meditation for many years, and who, he suggests, will have a greater energy output from their chakra centres. The results he has obtained are, however, viewed with a great deal of scepticism.

The chakras are thought to play an important role in health, from both a physical standpoint and an emotional or spiritual standpoint, as illness manifests itself not only in the aura but also in the chakras, through which the universal energy flows. Each chakras centre reacts to colour and sound. If the chakra centres are ill balanced or blocked, illness or general debility results, but this malaise works both ways, as our mental attitude can also affect the chakra centres.

There are seven main chakra centres, which lie along the line of the spinal column as shown in the diagram overleaf.

- The muladhara, base or root chakra, situated at the base of the spine, controls elimination.
- The svadisthana, spleen, sacral or abdomen chakra, situated close to the genital organs, controls sexual urges.
- The manipura chakra or solar plexus chakra, situated near the navel, controls digestion and the endocrine system.
- The anahat chakra or heart chakra, at the level of the heart, controls respiration and emotions.
- The visuddha chakra, thyroid or throat chakra, situated behind the throat, controls speech.
- The ajna chakra, third eye or brow chakra located between the eyebrows which controls the autonomous nervous system.
- The sahasrara, thousand-petalled lotus or crown chakra, situated at the top of the head, controls spiritual desires and is also connected with cerebral functions.

The Universal Power which we have already discussed enters the aura through the chakra at the top of the head, and works downwards through the other chakras, each centre using and changing the energy it receives according to the function which it governs.

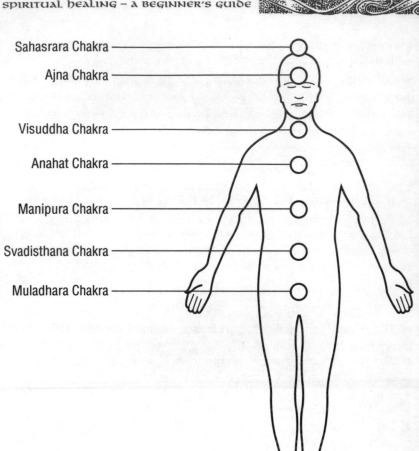

Sahasrara Chakra

Ajna Chakra

Visuddha Chakra

Anahat Chakra

Manipura Chakra

Svadisthana Chakra

Muladhara Chakra

Each chakra centre is responsible for a particular area of the body, and also emits colours. The base chakra will emit red, the spleen chakra orange, the solar plexus chakra yellow, the heart chakra green, the throat chakra blue, the brow chakra indigo and the crown chakra gold, white or violet.

WORKING WITH THE CHAKRA CENTRES

If you wish to work closely with the chakra centres as well as with the aura (the two being somewhat interrelated), you may wish to locate these centres yourself. One particularly good way of locating the chakra centres is radionics. However, many people will not have access to someone skilled in radionic diagnosis or healing, and so I would suggest that you might like to try dowsing using a pendulum.

EXERCISES IN DOWSING

For those unfamiliar with dowsing, you need to make a pendulum out of something natural; quartz crystal is a good idea with a leather string or thong attached, and you will need the co-operation of a friend as a willing volunteer on whom you can practise. There are many types and ways of making pendulums, discussed in both *Dowsing for beginners* and *Gems and Crystals for beginners* in this series. I would recommend both these books for further study about the chakra centres.

Having made or acquired a pendulum, hold it over your volunteer, who should ideally be facing magnetic north, and you will see how the pendulum sways in certain ways and in certain directions, clockwise, anticlockwise, backwards and forwards or sometimes just standing still (in which case no energy is apparant at that point at all). It is normally best, to start off with, if you concentrate on finding only one chakra centre at a time, and as the solar plexus chakra is normally the easiest to locate, start with that one.

As a rough guide to understanding what the various swings of your pendulum mean, I would suggest that you start by seeing which way the pendulum swings in answer to questions requiring a 'yes' or 'no' answer. This will tell you how your pendulum works with positives and negatives. After finding a 'yes' response, ask for a 'no' response as well as a 'don't know' – remember, though, to ask questions to which you know the answers! Once established, use the pendulum over the chakra centres, holding the pendulum in one hand, touching the various chakra points, and asking whether the chakra

centre is blocked or not. Watch which way the pendulum swings, and you will have your answer.

As you become more and more proficient with the pendulum, you will note how fast or slow the pendulum swings, indicating lots of energy or a reduction in energy emitted. You will also be able to pick up on the mental attitude of the person undergoing the experiment. Again, as with any experiment, please be aware that these things take time to perfect and understand. This is another case where it might take you a considerable time to understand exactly what it is you are picking up. You might also formulate your own ideas on what each chakra centre is telling you as you pass your pendulum over and around it.

Illnesses associated with each chakra centre

There are various illnesses and emotional problems said to relate specifically to blockages in each individual chakra centre, and these are listed below. In addition, we will discuss which colours will clear blockages or stimulate the centres. You can use these colours as visualisation tools when carrying out spiritual healing, or conversely use appropriately coloured crystals, or actively suggest that the person wears a particular colour.

Base or root chakra

Kidney or bladder problems, or problems with the process of elimination, obesity and with the lower back. Affected by fear, anger and sexual urge. Those with ME may have blockages here. Clear blockages using white light. Stimulate the chakra using red or orange. Practitioners of natural remedies often suggest this chakra can be balanced merely by standing on earth.

Spleen chakra

Digestive problems, reproductive problems, legs and feet. Affected by our sensitivities to others and those with lack of self-esteem or

motivation will have a blockage here, feeling confused or restless. Clear blockages with orange. Stimulate the chakra using green, blue or violet.

SOLAR PLEXUS CHAKRA

Heart problems, nervous difficulties or skin problems show here, as do stomach or kidney problems. Those people who repress their feelings often have blockages here. Clear blockages using blue or violet. Stimulate the chakra using yellow.

HEART CHAKRA

Immunity deficiency, circulation or breathing problems, also blood pressure or heart disease. Affected by anger and cleared by love. Clear blockages with indigo or red. Stimulate the chakra using green, rose or blue. It is said that if this chakra is open, all others will come into alignment with it.

THROAT CHAKRA

Thyroid problems, lympathic or oral problems, stiff neck, colds and flu, poor hearing, shoulders, arms and hands. Affected by lack of expression being allowed, stress, anxieties, fear and general negativities. Clear blockages with blue or violet. Also try using mantras, prayer and/or soothing music. Stimulate the chakra using red.

BROW CHAKRA

Migraine headaches, ear and eye problems, sinusitis. Also problems with the pituitary gland. Affected by fear, worry and doubts. Clear blockages with green. Stimulate the chakra using indigo or blue.

CROWN CHAKRA

Seasonal depression (SAD), depression or lack of mental clarity, boredom, confusion, brain problems. Affected by selfishness. Clear blockages with gold or indigo. Stimulate the chakra using white.

EXERCISES TO PRACTISE

Before reading the next chapter, practise the exercises we have already covered on relaxation and breathing, satisfy yourself that you feel comfortable and happy with these, and then progress to practising, both on yourself and on other people, seeing and detecting the aura and chakra centres. I really would not suggest at this stage that you try to balance or stimulate the chakra centres or work actively on the aura. It is sufficient, at this stage, just to feel comfortable with what we have learned before progressing. All these things take a lot of time, effort and practice before they become second nature. Take your time, and remember that everything we have learned to date needs a relaxed frame of mind to start off with. Practise relaxation. If you can, try to get into that alpha state each day, for at least twenty minutes.

CHAPTER 5

POSITIVE Thoughts

In Chapter 1, we briefly discussed the link between mind and body, what is medically called psychoneuroimmunology, and it is now necessary to delve into the subject a little further in order that we can start to heal ourselves and other people, if we choose to do so. We need to know how to be positive, not just for ourselves, but to help others – we will discuss how to visualise positive outcomes for seemingly difficult circumstances, we will also discuss how this positive mental attitude can help us all to feel better in ourselves. The power of prayer and affirmations will also be discussed, as most spiritual healers will open their treatments with prayer, and end with prayer for continued help to be given to the patient until the next healing treatment can be given.

Illness and mental thought

We have already considered how a negative attitude can affect any healing given, and briefly considered what a negative attitude can cause, both in symptoms and in actual illness, but I want to reinforce this, in order that we can all be totally aware of what negativities do to us.

I do not wish to dwell unnecessarily on this subject or quote statistics which may cause undue concern, but following research carried out in the USA by Dr Lawrence LeShan and Dr Carl Simonton, there has

been shown to be a positive link between negative mental states and certain types of cancer. Low personal esteem, an inability to show anger, extreme and unreleased tension, a tendency towards resentment and self-pity and the inability to forgive people have all been shown to link with a higher incidence of cancer in future years. In addition, it is widely accepted that those suffering from high levels of stress and tension are likely to develop high blood pressure and suffer more from heart disease than other groups with similar lifestyles. Basically, the bottom line is that we need to reduce all these negativities, and cope with them effectively when they do occur in order to stay well.

We have already discussed the power of love and the universal energies. We have seen how strong this power is, and what wonderful healing it can accomplish. At one time or another, we all feel down and miserable, but we need to strive to rise above this. Negative feelings of guilt, remorse, anger, etc. are all right in their place – but we have to put these things into perspective, and not allow them to become dominant parts of our lives. If you like, we need to be kind to ourselves by being positive with our emotions.

It is important to realise that, as Edgar Cayce said many times in his work *Mind is the Builder*, we can change our attitudes, and by so doing, we can also start to change our health.

We should start by working on things which are easier to change. You will recall we discussed anger, and how to let such things wash over us in an earlier chapter. We need to learn to be patient, both with ourselves and with others. Not everyone works in the same way, or at the same speed, and we have to accept that we are all different. We should also try to realise that nobody possesses or owns anybody else. We are all able to make up our own minds, and jealously and possessiveness really should have no part in our behaviour. Likewise, we need to understand what it is to forgive, both ourselves and other people, and learn to try not to judge others – as it says in the Bible in Luke 6 'judge not and you will not be judged'. Likewise in John 8 we hear Jesus's words 'Let him who is without sin cast the first stone'. None of us is perfect, and it is not up to us to judge other people by our standards or by any others. By

trying not to be so hard on ourselves as a first step, we will in turn learn not to be so hard on others.

CAN WE ACHIEVE HEALING BY USING THE POWER OF THE MIND?

The power of the mind is a great thing. Technological advances have provided us with really brilliant computers and virtual reality systems which can give information at the touch of a button, but none of these systems can compare with the power of the mind – our brain is the best computer we are ever likely to come across.

In recent years, there has been a huge growth in the 'human potential movement', and in what is called transpersonal psychology. I believe that if we learn to use our minds to their fullest potential, we can accomplish many things which would, previously, have seemed impossible. Once we feel we can do something, we normally can, unless of course, our expectations are ridiculous and totally unattainable to start off with. There are some things we really can't alter. It would be a totally futile exercise for me to visualise waking up and being six inches taller, even though I would love to be taller than I am. I am just not going to grow any more. Things like that only happen in movies. I have to accept that, so we need to set goals which we feel we can attain.

All we need to do is learn how to be positive, and learn how to visualise positive outcomes to situations. We can do a lot to speed up the healing process and produce changes in our physical state by mind power alone. This mental attitude is all part and parcel of helping ourselves, as it is totally wrong to be reliant upon anybody else without being prepared to accept some of the responsibility ourselves.

CREATIVE VISUALISATION

We are going to start to think about positive visualisation, or what is sometimes known as creative visualisation. You may think this is

something which can be achieved only in a state of meditation. When we carry out relaxation techniques, we often use visualisation as an aid, but it doesn't stop there, because we all use visualisation in some form or other, even if only rarely. You might also have the misconception that creative visualisation is the same as casting a spell and has something to do with witchcraft or magic. What we are talking about is the power of imagination and the greater power of the mind. We are not talking about deciding that you really need a new car, visualising it and creating mind power so that you get it. We are talking about changing negative situations, of which disease is one, into something more positive, using visualisation as a technique. We are talking about positive thinking, nothing weird or odd. Creative imagery has been used over countless centuries, especially in the East, and features in the philosophies of most ancient cultures, and indeed of many tribal histories.

Creative visualisation is something which needs to emphasise the positive, rather than the negative. Most of us would agree that if we go out to a party not really wanting to go, we inevitably don't enjoy ourselves, and it would have been a lot better to have stayed at home. What happened was that we mentally turned what could have been a happy occasion into something that wasn't, because we didn't want a happy outcome. If we had gone out thinking we were going to enjoy ourselves, even if we couldn't actually say we were likely to have a great time, the chances are we would have come back feeling reasonably happy. I suppose it goes back to the 'Is the glass half full or half empty' rationale.

Taking another scenario, let's think about creative visualisation and the body, something which we have actually already covered, although perhaps you might not have realised this. We have learned to relax. We take ourselves off to somewhere quiet, and practise the exercises in relaxation and breathing which we have already discussed. Relaxation and being relaxed is important for the technique to be effective. Let's further pretend that we have a cold. Using the technique of creative visualisation we imagine our cold as, say, an iceberg. We imagine that we can see this iceberg melting. Slowly but surely, it is reducing in size, until eventually it is nearly gone. We finish our relaxation time, and get up and carry on with our everyday business.

You might say, 'So what? What is that likely to have achieved? You may be relaxed but that's about it'. You would be wrong. It has been shown by many healers, especially British healer Matthew Manning, that such techniques really do produce positive results, a reduction in symptoms and also often a reduction in disease. However, you need to feel happy with that. If you don't, you are already thinking negatively, and the whole exercise would be futile.

Creative visualisation is really quite a logical thing, not something merely associated with yogis or mystics, which many people assume. Basically, all that creative visualisation relies upon is an element of imagination in the first place, but a maintenance of logic, positivity and optimism throughout. It is nothing mystic, nothing 'out of this world', but merely the power of the mind, linked into the individual cells of the body. It is also something of which mankind has been aware for many centuries, although it gained more popularity following the books published by Norman Peale. In his book *The Power of Positive Thinking*, published in 1952, Peale suggested that a combination of prayer, faith in God, a positive frame of mind and affirmations could produce a positive response. We will be looking at both prayer and affirmations later, but this concept is something that many complementary therapists will agree upon. In fact, there are many working within the complementary health field who will suggest that every thought you think creates your future.

If you think about it, we are all capable of making visual images. We do so most nights when we dream. All we have to do is to make such visual images while we are still awake – like a sort of positive daydream. You may remember that in Chapter 2 we discussed how the ancient Greeks and Egyptians actively encouraged people with illnesses to go into the healing temples to sleep, and perhaps dream positively that healing was taking place. You may also recall how Paracelsus linked the power of the mind, or imagination, and the power to cause and cure illness. Creative visualisation is nothing new.

Matthew Manning actively uses creative visualisation techniques in his work with patients. However, he has noticed through this work that once people try too hard, little is achieved. If, however, they try less, and concentration is broken every now and again, more is achieved.

This is called The Law of Reversed Effort, a term coined by the Frenchman Burnheim. It has been demonstrated many times that the harder you try, the less successful you become. For example, if you plant a bulb, and are forever digging it up, it will never grow. If you try really hard to concentrate on getting better, or on a visualisation being perfect, the chances are it won't happen, and you will end up feeling worse.

Some years ago, there was an advert on British television for a type of sweet which was said to have been 'made to make your mouth water'. I remember being intrigued by the advert, as at the time I was studying psychology, part of which was the study of Pavlov and experiments he carried out on dogs. Pavlov showed dogs various food substances to see how anticipation made them salivate. He called this process Unconditional Stimulus. It seemed to me that this advert was saying the same thing, and without it being a conscious decision, I discovered that watching the advert made saliva flow into my mouth. As a result, even now, I cannot think of the advert without my mouth filling with saliva – mental thoughts have created a bodily reaction.

Tests carried out to show the link between mental image and bodily functions in humans have probably been done for many years, but one such famous test was carried out in the early 1920s in America. Edmund Jacobson discovered that when a man visualised himself running while in a state of relaxation, his leg muscles would twitch involuntarily.

As part of many of his healing treatments, one of Matthew Manning's early techniques involves asking patients to think of biting into a lemon, in order to convince them of the link between mind and body. Most people will salivate as this point, and he will then explain to them that they have shown that creative visualisation can work on bodily functions. At this point, they feel more comfortable with the concept, and further visualisation techniques can be worked through.

I have read many reports of the work Manning has carried out, including studies on cancer patients. In many such cases, he suggests to the patient concerned that they see their cancer cells being 'zapped' by white light, the ultimate healing colour. Other techniques he uses include asking cancer patients to visualise, order and instruct their white blood cells, which are the body's own defence system, to become

so active and strong that they can overcome the disease. Other healers suggest ships coming along and taking the disease out to sea, or similar thoughts, and it has been shown by Dr Carl Simonton in tests carried out over many years in America that in many cases, a remission of disease is achieved, or in some cases the disease seems to disappear altogether, and within the USA, Simonton has become somewhat of a pioneer for visualisation techniques, along with Dr Bernie Siegel.

TAKING RESPONSIBILITY

Whatever form of creative visualisation technique is used, it has to be something with which the person concerned feels comfortable. It also has to be accepted by the patient that they themselves are taking part of the responsibility for the healing being given, and that they need to adopt a different attitude to their disease.

It would be totally useless to ask someone who is totally against any form of aggression to visualise their disease being attacked by a Japanese Samurai Warrior. It would, in such cases, be better to suggest that the body's own energy system, which we could perhaps link to a gentle stream is merely carrying the disease out of the body and out to sea. It is generally accepted that the immune system can be altered by thoughts and feelings, and so this visualisation only reinforces something which medical science is able to accept. It would also be totally pointless for a person to carry out creative visualisation if they are not happy with the whole process or if they refuse to help themselves, which goes back to those people who really don't want to be well, or to alter their lifestyles, diet or whatever as a side issue. Matthew Manning has gone as far as suggesting that up to 40 per cent of people who come to him asking for healing decide that they don't want to know and consequently follow through with it, because he makes it clear from the start that they must also be prepared to help themselves, rather than be totally reliant upon his help as a healer.

For the process to be successful, the patients have to create an image with which they feel comfortable, which must be clear, and created or agreed upon by the patients concerned for themselves. If a suggestion is made with which someone doesn't feel too happy, most healers will

ask the patient to find his or her own image. It is much better for patients to understand that they are in charge, rather than feeling that they are being told what to do, feel, see, etc. At the end of the day, we are talking about their bodies, in the same way as we ourselves are dealing with ours. You can make suggestions, but nobody has the right to tell another person what to think or to do.

If we have problems even imagining mental images, it is often the case that we haven't really given ourselves the permission to do so. Some people feel that is simply selfish and totally wrong to try to do anything to change 'fate'. I would disagree. There is nothing wrong with helping the body to help itself, and that is all we are endeavouring to do with creative visualisation. If, when using creative visualisation techniques for health benefits, we think less of becoming totally well and think more of becoming a little better, our expectations change, become more within the realms of possibility, and more is achieved as a result. If you start anything thinking that you can't possibly win, you won't. We all have to permanently review our goal posts, bringing them nearer if we need to, or when things are going well, moving them a little further away.

Some people have a problem holding on to a visualisation. If you are one of these people, you may want to think about recording your own tape, so that you can listen to your own voice (much better than thinking that someone else, alien to you, is telling you what to do), and see if that works for you. You will have to make some sort of script, or plan of what you are going to say and what you are hoping to achieve, but other than that, all you need is a tape-recorder and some time. It is also important to be positive throughout if you are doing this, either for yourself or other people. Don't use negative phrases. Be positive in all your statements. If you say to people 'I would prefer you not to think of ...' they invariably forget the word 'not' and then think of whatever it is you would prefer them to disregard. As someone said to me once when explaining this, 'Don't say don't'. It is also worthwhile using the phrase 'You want to be well', rather than the phrase 'You would like to feel better'. If you think you want something, you are far more likely to get it. If you just think you would like something, the emphasis isn't so great.

There are many types of visualisation techniques which we could discuss for you to try, and some suggestions will be given at the end of the chapter. There are other techniques to try mentioned in *Visualisation for beginners*, in this series. Furthering the thought of positive thinking, we also need to consider positive affirmations – statements we can make to ourselves at any time to reinforce our positivity.

Affirmations

What is an affirmation? You may think it is something which Buddhists use as part of their meditation – repetition of the phrase 'Om' for example to stop the mind wandering off. This isn't an affirmation but a chant, and we will be discussing both mantras and chants later. Basically, we are talking about merely the act of affirming to ourselves that we are getting better. It is nothing mystical or magic, but something which expresses optimism.

Affirmation is also known as Coueism after Frenchman Emile Coué, (1857–1926) who developed the technique at the end of the nineteenth century following similar work by Liebault before him. We are going to learn how focusing our minds on the affirmation 'Every day, in every way, I am getting better and better' can help to speed up the healing process. This form of autosuggestion, when linked with healing, positive thought, creative visualisation and relaxation, can and does produce a reduction in illness and disease. Basically, the repetition of a positive phrase makes an impression upon our imagination, and then the imagination or subconscious sets to work to carry out the phrase, meaning reduction in pain, tension, and anxiety as well as physical disease.

Coué was an apothecary, and became increasingly interested in the relationship between mind and body. Assessing the work of doctors who used hypnotism, he began to formulate his own ideas. He felt that doctors took far too little notice of the power of the imagination, and noted that hypnotism worked only because of the power of the autosuggestion.

Realising that people who really didn't think they would recover from an illness often didn't, Coué devoted much of his life to developing and teaching his techniques.

Coué believed that if his phrase, which was seen as a command or order, was repeated during relaxation, preferably just before falling asleep and just after waking up, it becomes implanted in the mind and as such the body's own energy forces could be directed to restore harmony and reduce disease. Coué suggested that this phrase be repeated about twenty times, either silently or aloud. That is not a specific instruction. There is no magic associated with it. Twenty times has been shown to be just about the right number for the mind to register it at a deep level. You may wish to try this on yourself over a period of time, to see how it works for you, before trying it out on other people, or even suggesting that they use it. At the end of the day, if you are convinced that it works for you, you will be more convincing when explaining it to other people. Anyway, you shouldn't just take my word for it, or Coué's for that matter. You must try it out for yourself.

You may be thinking of using your own phrase. I would advise against this at this stage. During his early experiments, Coué used various phrases, such as 'My leg is mending' but found that, by modifying this and broadening it to 'Every day, ...', it became more acceptable, because specifics were taken away. Let's take the example of the broken leg. Unless we are medically trained, we will not know how the various components of the leg work with each other for healing to be complete. We may just assume we are dealing with a broken bone, but even then, there is far more to the mending of a broken bone than we may be aware. If we realise that we don't have to know what is wrong to put it right, but merely ask that things get better, we won't fall foul of making mistakes – our diagnoses might have been wrong, for example, or we might have just caused our minds to concentrate on the physical symptom or pain, rather than on the positive outcome.

As with visualisation techniques, it is also important not to use negatives. Rather than saying 'I haven't got a headache' which is likely to make you focus more on the fact that you have got a headache,

and thus make it worse, think of a positive statement. One affirmation you might like to consider experimenting with in relaxation is 'I am completely at peace and totally relaxed.' I have used this phrase with much success.

Since Coué's time, many other forms of positive affirmation techniques have been developed. One of these is the Silva Method, so called after Jose Silva, who developed the therapy in the 1960s.

So are affirmations prayers? When we pray, are we merely stating something for it to be registered at a deeper level in our minds? I think not, but many people who are unhappy with prayer as a concept may disagree. We have already briefly discussed the power of prayer and charismatic healing, but need to delve a little more into this deeply spiritual practice.

The power of prayer

Whether you believe in God, or in something less personal, you will know about prayer. All of us know about prayer, irrespective of any religious or spiritual background. We might not all actively pray, and we may not all pray in the same way, but we all know of and are familiar with the concept of prayer.

I fully appreciate that there are many people who do not believe in God. These people might like to think of prayers as thoughts, expressed either silently or given voice, and once you appreciate that the power of thought and the power of the mind are extremely strong, irrespective of whether you believe in God, you can accept that prayers, as thoughts, are important. Even if you think of prayers only as means of expressing your hopes and fears, you should understand that the act of prayer, of focusing your attention on situations which concern you, is a good thing.

Prayers do work. I firmly believe in the power of prayer, and you may recall that we discussed how Sir Francis Chichester credited his recovery from lung cancer to the power of prayer, or what is now known as charismatic healing. Anybody can pray, anywhere, at any time, alone or with other people. You don't have to be of a particular

faith, religion, colour or creed to pray. We can all pray. All that is needed is for the person praying to believe that their prayer is heard, to have faith, and to believe that it will be answered. Prayer can cover any distance (so we can pray about people who may be on the other side of the world), it can be personal or impersonal, it can be short or long – prayer is a very versatile thing!

You might feel that prayer is a waste of time, because, as far as you are concerned, your prayers never seem to be answered, but are you really praying properly? Are you sincerely asking for help? Are you perhaps praying for something you don't really want, just to 'test the waters?' Are you praying to someone or something which, deep down, you don't believe in? Prayers are personal things, and should be from the heart to someone or something in which you believe.

You might also feel that you have to go to a church to pray, or be party to a religious ceremony. You might think that you have to pray on your knees with your hands together. While it is a good idea to pray on our own, the power of group prayer is a great thing. It isn't a prerequisite that we are in a church or anywhere else for that matter. What we are doing when we pray is asking for help and saying thanks for help given. That can be done anywhere, and be done either alone or with others.

When we were children, we turned to our parents with our worries and fears. Often, they did little other than listen, but we felt better, because even if they didn't immediately respond, we felt that we had shared the problem, it was safe with them, and that ultimately we might receive the help we felt was warranted. Sometimes, all we wanted to do was to confess about something we had done wrong. If you think about it, the same can be said of prayer. When we pray, we are asking for help, asking forgiveness and/or asking for a favour, unlike meditation when we are not asking for anything. We are, according to the Christian model prayer or 'Lord's prayer', praying to 'Our Father, in heaven'. We are, then, praying to our ultimate parent. When we pray, we should just imagine that we are talking to someone close and in whom we can trust.

So what do I mean by prayers? One thing I don't mean is the repetition of something without thought, as if by rote. Most Christians know the

model or 'Lord's prayer', but how many actually take time to think about it as they pray. More often than not, it is just churned out. For any prayer to be effective, we have to think about it. It isn't just a mantra. Neither do I think that prayers should just ask for something. They should also give thanks, and not be confined to things which we want, either for ourselves or for others. From a healing angle, all we are doing is asking for and earnestly desiring to be made well or to be healed.

The Bible tells us much about prayer. It explains to us that we should never feel abandoned or anxious over anything, and that praying will help us (Philippians 4). It tells Christians that prayers are best directed to God through Jesus. In the model prayer, we are advised to ask for help for ourselves, and by using the word 'us', rather than 'me', we are including other people. We aren't confining our prayer just to ourselves – we aren't being selfish and thinking only of ourselves, our own interests and desires.

Dr Larry Dossey is one person who has actively studied the power of prayer and its relationship to good health. In test situations in San Francisco, patients in a coronary care unit who prayed and were prayed for seemed to need less medical help than those who did not pray and were not prayed for. The actual statistic was that out of 393 coronary patients, those who prayed and were prayed for were five times less likely than the others to require antibiotics and three times less likely than the others to develop pulmonary edema. Similarly, in a discussion on television, José Carreras, the opera singer, said he firmly believed that his recovery from leukaemia had been due in great part not only to his prayers, but to the prayers from people around the world, which he linked in to the power of their love for him, even though many of the people had probably never met him, and never would.

Larry Dossey and his colleagues have shown that prayers work on all life forms, and not just on humans. They have further shown that prayers don't have to be done in a special way.

At the start of most spiritual healing treatments, there will be an opening prayer. Likewise, at the end of a treatment, prayer will be given as a form of thanks for the help received, and asking for

continued help to be given until the next healing treatment is given. I would seriously recommend anybody intending to carry out spiritual healing to follow this suggested format.

We have already seen that affirmations are not prayers. Prayers are different things. But are prayers the same as chants, and are chants the same as mantras?

Chants and Mantras

Chants are normally things involving religious ceremony, rites or rituals, and can be thought of as devotional things. Chanting may be looked upon as something which only Eastern groups practise, and there are, in fact, three Eastern forms of chanting – the Byzantine, Syrian and Armenian. Those familiar with Gregorian chants may already be thinking in terms of a religious thing, and chanting of the name of Jesus in prayer was recommended by Diadochus of Photice in the middle of the fifth century, and by John Climacus in the early seventh century. This developed into various Christian chants, including Western forms, Gregorian, Gallican, Mozarabic and Ambrosian.

Chants can also be done as part of a meditation process, and are normally done with a rhythm. Many sectors of society actively use chants, feeling that these help to raise the consciousness of the participants, such as the Buddhists, Hindus and Muslims. Various Hindu and Buddhist groups use 'Om' as it represents Brahman, while other Buddhists will use the name Buddha as a chant, suggesting that this will alleviate the necessity for them to reincarnate and allow then to join Buddha. Followers of Islam will chant the ninety-nine names of Allah.

Mantras, on the other hand, are normally phrases or even words which tend to have no actual meaning. The Hare Krishna singers constantly repeat mantras to concentrate their minds on to one point, but most mantras are silent.

Mantras are also used in transcendental meditation, in which the mantra is not deliberately repeated. Students of TM are trained in a

technique which allows the mantra to repeat itself until another appears. Between losing the mantra and awaiting the next one, a state of pure consciousness is said to be achieved.

With mantras, and to some degree with chants used for a similar purpose, the free will of the person is not involved. The mind is not focused on an ultimate goal, for example healing of the body.

Chants and mantras may not be part of spiritual healing to most of us, but it is worthwhile pointing out that to various American Indian people, chanting is vitally important to healing treatment. In fact, some Navajo will not accept conventional medical treatment without an accompanying chant, or what they call chantaways. Feeling that chantaways restore harmony, Navajo legend suggests that the instruction to chantaways was given to them by The Holy Ones, unseen spirits such as The Wind People.

EXERCISE IN VISUALISATION

Some people may feel that they can go immediately on to creative visualisation linked to healing, while others may wish to try this exercise. Remember, this visualisation is only a suggestion. You can choose to practise your own if you wish to. There are no rules here, only guidelines.

First, you must feel confident in your ability to relax. You need to be mentally relaxed and physically relaxed, so I suggest you run over the techniques we have already discussed before progressing. If you feel unhappy at that stage, don't progress until you are. You may want to record yourself talking this through, or conversely you may feel confident enough just to think yourself through it. It is your decision.

Go through the relaxation techniques we have discussed. Once relaxed, imagine that you can see a brick wall. That brick wall is painted white. You can see each brick and you can see only the wall. Imagine that you see a small hole in that brick wall. It is only a little hole, but as you look through it, you can see a field beyond. You really like the look of the field. You want to be in that field, rather than stuck

in front of the brick wall. You decide to try to enlarge the hole in the wall. Little by little you take away cement, mortar, bricks – you really want to make a hole to climb through. This takes time. You may not find yourself able to get through the hole in the first go. You might find that you can get through the hole in the first session. If you are lucky enough to be able to get through the hole, you will find yourself in that field. Everything there is perfect. The wall is behind you. You are somewhere warm, you feel happy, relaxed and at peace. You will never go back to the wall. You have no need. Stay in that visualisation for as long as you can before coming back to 'the real world'.

Basically what we have done is use the brick wall to symbolise your problems or your illness or your state of mind. By breaking through that wall, you have managed to leave your problems behind. You have broken through to happiness, and know that you will never return to the problem.

This is a simplistic exercise, and you may wish to use your own analogies. Again, it is a personal thing, and I will leave that with you. However, if you are intending to use creative visualisation in your healing, of either yourself or of others, I really would advise you to practise for a while to be sure you feel confident with the techniques, how it all works, and what outcome can be achieved. This is another case where things cannot be rushed. Similarly, if you are intending to use affirmations, or Coué's affirmation, do practise for a while on yourself before suggesting it to anybody else. Don't take anybody's word for something unless you have tried it yourself, and ultimately feel happy with it.

6 hEALING OURSELVES

In this chapter, we are going to start to look at healing ourselves by changes in lifestyle and diet. If we are hoping ever to be in a position to advise or help other people, we have to look at our own lifestyles and diet and make corrections where necessary. After all, if you had diabetes linked directly to being overweight, would you for example, follow a diet plan if the person telling you about it was grossly overweight and didn't follow it themselves? We also need to take a look how at we can practise healing, both on ourselves and on others. Before starting healing on anybody else, we really have to be confident that we are capable of understanding what we are doing, and I would strongly suggest that you confine any experiments you wish to conduct to members of your family or close friends, rather than anybody else. It takes many years to become a skilled and proficient healer. Try out your newly acquired knowledge on yourself as a first step, then progress to family and friends, who must be willing, not press-ganged!

LOOKING AT OUR LIFESTYLE

It is a great thing if we can see ourselves as others see us. More often than not, we can't, or perhaps we don't want to. There comes a point in our lives when we just have to take responsibility for ourselves. At that point in time, we take an objective look, see things which need altering, and try positively to do something about that.

I firmly believe that all healing starts with self-healing. If you knew, for example, that eating fatty foods caused you gastric problems, you would be silly if you kept eating fried food, or things high in fat content. Lots of people do just that though, and then wonder why they are always feeling ill.

For many years, I have been actively advising people on altering their lifestyle to feel better about themselves. Sometimes people take up my suggestions, but at the end of the day I can't be with them all the time, and there comes a point when they have to start to stand on their own two feet and do something for themselves. Other people I come across claim that they really want to be well, to be healthy, yet are unwilling to do anything at all to bring about that goal. I have spent many hours with people who tell me how unhappy they are, how they want to be well, how they fully appreciate that their weight problems or lifestyle are contributing to their ill health, but then won't do anything at all to change the situation. At that point, there is nothing further I can do. People must have to really want to do something for themselves. I have lost count of the number of times I've heard someone say 'It's OK for you – you are so positive. If you were with me all the time, it would be so much easier.' I can't be with clients all day long. They must learn for themselves.

If a person really wants to be well, having appreciated the link between mind and body, between what we eat and what we are, between what exercise we do and our stamina levels and so on, and then chooses to do nothing about that imbalance, he or she will never learn to aid the healing process, and consequently, any visit to a healer is unlikely to achieve results.

If you know you are under a great deal of stress and do nothing to alter your schedule to create a slot in it for you, you are merely perpetuating a problem. If you have never tried relaxation techniques before, you might not find it easy to start off with, but at least give it a try. Likewise, if you have come to appreciate the strong link between mental attitude and bodily functions or illness, and have never tried affirmations or creative visualisation, please try.

I have certain guidelines which I try to use in my own daily life. I believe that they work because they work for me, and I know that

they have worked for other people I have suggested them to. If you really truly feel that you want to feel better in yourself, try them out.

Daily suggestions for a healthier life

EATING

Your body is like a machine. It needs energy to work. We provide that energy in the form of food and drink. However, we have to take a positive look at the sort of food we eat. Unfortunately, there is a growing dependence upon convenience and 'fast foods' because of the speed of our lives. We seem to need to eat quickly, haven't got the time (or the inclination) to take time over preparing our food, and so eat processed food rather than fresh natural products. Most of these foods are high in fat content. If you think that fat contains more than twice as many calories as protein and carbohydrate, you can then start to see why eating foods with a high fat content increases the chances that we will in turn become fat or fatter.

Make sure that you have something to eat before you leave the house for work. Cereal is great, or try yogurt or fresh fruit. Don't think in terms of a fried breakfast.

Make time for a proper lunch. Don't eat on the run. Sit down, take your time and concentrate on what you are eating. Make your lunch an important part of your day, as it will re-fuel your body and give you the energy for the afternoon, until you can eat again. Try to avoid things which you know to be high in fat. Try to have some protein but don't make meat the main part of your meal. Make sure you have lots of vegetables and carbohydrates, such as potatoes, rice or pasta. Be careful about sauces. Try to have fruit afterwards if you can.

For your evening meal, as your body is unlikely to be using much energy in the evening, try to eat less than perhaps you would otherwise have done. Again, think about fat content, and make sure you sit down to eat, preferably not in front of the television, as often you won't be concentrating sufficiently on what you are eating, and then, because it hasn't registered in your mind, in a few hours time you will feel hungry again.

Try not to snack. Most snacks are high in fat: most crisps are 65 per cent fat; peanuts are even worse. Start looking at the labels of the products you buy. If the fat content is more than 30 per cent of the total calories, avoid the product. If you have a problem with eating, maybe you might like to know that much of the disease we have is exacerbated by being overweight, and in some cases, as in the case of diabetes, can be caused by being overweight.

People who understand the effect that colour has on our lives also suggest that when we are run down or feeling below par, we should think about taking food into our systems the colour of which links to high energy. A good example of this is carrots – orange and red are energy colours, and at Bristol Cancer Centre, a great deal of emphasis is placed on eating fresh products with bright colours.

DRINKING

We all need to drink to replace our fluid levels. Most of us don't drink anything like the amount we should. I know that I have to really think hard about drinking enough, and am as guilty as many in drinking the wrong things. We discussed water earlier on, and we should all drink far more water than we do. Tea and coffee are all well and good, but the caffeine content of these drinks, and in soft drinks, really isn't that good for us, as caffeine is a stimulant. Water will help flush the system of impurities and contains all the necessary minerals the body needs. Try to drink more water. Also think about alcohol input, how much you drink and why you do it. Most people have a drink to unwind. Alcohol will help you unwind, but alcohol is also a toxin. The body has to work twice as hard after you have been drinking to rid itself of the toxins. If you drink when you eat, the body will automatically work hard to deal with the toxins rather than on dealing with what you are eating, resulting in many cases in fat deposits being laid down, rather than in fat being used up.

EXERCISE

If we eat more in calories than we burn off, we will put on weight. If we eat only 150 calories a week more than we burn off, we will end up nearly 2½ lbs heavier by the end of the year.

Try walking more than you probably have done. You can relax while walking, and it is a great form of exercise, and often helps to clear the head. By walking, I don't mean at a window-shopping speed, I mean walking at a reasonable pace. Most people in the UK find it a problem to walk a mile in twenty minutes. You should aim to be able to walk a mile in fourteen minutes maximum. Everybody in the UK would be a lot healthier if they all walked an additional twenty minutes a day, rain or shine.

If you want to meet people, think about joining a club or organisation which includes exercise in its programme. Exercise can be quite a social thing, and doesn't mean being drenched in sweat. For exercise to be effective, we should all be able to hold a conversation as we exercise – this is called the talk test.

Part of my job includes working with people who have been referred by their doctor because they are suffering with stress, high blood pressure, various heart problems and/or are overweight. Many of those people were frightened to death at the though of doing any exercise at all, but stuck with it, and all of them have told me, either as a group or individually, that they all feel better for including exercise as part of their daily regime. In nice weather make sure you do some exercise outside. The Greeks and other ancient civilisations and groups, such as the Essenes, appreciated the body's need for sunshine, and the current 'discovery' of SAD (feeling low and lifeless at times when there is no natural sunshine) reinforces the necessity for a little bit of sunshine on our skins. Notice, I say a little bit. I am not talking about becoming tanned, which is another topic for discussion altogether.

RELAXATION

We need to programme in time for ourselves. One of the most difficult things to do, especially in a family situation, is to find time for ourselves, when we can be on our own and relax. More often than not, especially for women, the only time for relaxation is when the kids are in bed, late at night. At that stage, all most people do is sit and watch television. That isn't what I mean by relaxation. I mean finding time, on your own, to unwind and fully relax. If you find difficulty carrying out relaxation techniques, at least take yourself off to the bathroom and have a long relaxing bath, with some nice smelling oils and some relaxing music. Learn to breathe rather than just take in oxygen. If you don't think you can motivate yourself to relax, join a relaxation group or find a yoga teacher. Yoga is a great way of helping the body to unwind. If you want to try something a little different, look for groups teaching autogenics, art therapy, Gestalt therapy or another form or complementary healing through relaxation and reduction in tension.

LIFESTYLE

If you smoke, try to give up. I am very anti-smoking, probably because smoking was given as the cause for my husband's death through cancer, and also led to my mother developing emphysema from which she died. If you think you are immune to disease through smoking, think again. I have seen what it does to people and I wouldn't wish that on anybody. Not only are smokers killing themselves, but through passive smoking, many others are becoming ill. Pollution is a killer. It all goes back to responsibility, personal responsibility as well as being responsible for other people – remember 'No man is an island'.

Make sure that you have adequate clothing on in cold weather. If that sounds condescending, it isn't meant to, but just take a look at the amount of people who walk around in really cold weather with thin clothing on. Is it any wonder we fall foul of so many colds? Think also of wearing natural fibres.

If you know you suffer with stress, and that you need space for yourself, try to programme it in. Sounds easy, but I know it isn't. You are important – not only to yourself, but to family and friends. If you are stressed all the time, you are likely to get angry easily, feel permanently tense, and be working on overdrive. Try to look objectively at your programme for the day, and do something which will reduce stress. Do something daily. If you become ill through stress, nothing is achieved other than ill health. Make a positive effort to ensure that illness through stress is something which won't happen to you.

EMOTIONS AND ATTITUDE

Let situations of tension wash over you a little. Most of us have to work on that all the time. It is all so easy to 'rise to the bait' and become tense, angry or whatever. Step back from situations if you can. In the Bible, Proverbs 17, it states 'Before the quarrel has burst forth, take your leave'. I remember someone saying once that they had just saved themselves from a really stressful situation. When I enquired as to what they had done, all they said was 'I left the room'. It often takes far more courage to walk away than to stand and fight, so don't assume that by walking away you have been weak. Conflict is all about manipulation and misuse of energy. Physical dominance takes away mental clarity, and feeds on insecurities and weaknesses. It also kills love. We have no need to compete with each other and get involved in power struggles. Try to live in harmony with other people, however hard that may be.

Learn to talk problems and difficulties through, rather than bottling them up inside. Realise that other people are entitled to their viewpoints, however different from yours they may be, and respect the fact that they have a right to their opinions, and an equal right to voice them. If you feel they are really wrong, tell them in a nice way. Don't, however, impose your opinion or your will on other people. It leads to resentment. Remember that we all have our own path to travel, and don't let other people control you, or in turn try to control other people. Be yourself, and know yourself.

Don't assume just because you have studied something that you have all the answers. Taking an example, having books on cooking doesn't make you a chef. We continue to learn throughout our lives. If someone genuinely wants to help others, that person must also realise that he or she might not have all the answers. It isn't a sign of weakness to say that you don't know something. It's just being honest.

Actively tell people how much they mean to you. Don't just assume that they know because often they don't, or think that because you buy presents every now and again, this is enough. Many of us need reassurance that we are loved and needed, even though we may know this deep down anyway. Someone told me once that if we were all hugged and kissed each day, we would live longer as a result. Give it a go. You haven't got anything to lose.

Learn from mistakes you have made in the past, and let go of outmoded ideas. Try not to keep going down the same track again and again. Also learn from the mistakes of your parents and don't perpetuate their mistakes or incorrect attitudes.

Remember that the universe is composed of energy. Learn to see it. See the energy in trees and plants, and learn about our own energy fields. Try to live close to Nature and in accord with it, rather than against it, and try to preserve what humans haven't already destroyed, through greed or ignorance. Practise using the energy we have available to us from the higher source as a means of ending conflict, both emotional and physical, and use it in a healing capacity, both on yourself and on other people with whom you come into contact. Learn to love unconditionally. Love is a powerful energy.

Try to be positive, but don't be too hard on yourself, and know that you will occasionally get the balance wrong. Listen to your thoughts, and if you are slipping into negativity, try to change it round. Look for the good in situations and in other people, however hard that may be, and concentrate on the positive rather than the negative aspects of everything.

Live your life for you, and don't live your life through other people, as it will be to your detriment. Don't look for what you personally lack in someone else, and expect that they will make you a whole

person. Find that missing link in yourself, and develop yourself as a person, rather than drawing from them. Be truthful with yourself, as well as with others. Identify your own shortcomings and work on those, rather than concentrating too much on the shortcomings of other people.

Try to live a spiritual life, following perhaps the example of Jesus if you have Christian beliefs. I firmly believe that we will all live a truly spiritual life eventually, and actively look forward to that time. Create that future life by living that way now, and other people will follow your example – they call it the domino effect. It takes only twelve people to change a nation, so they say. Be one of the twelve.

All these things will help you as a person, as a potential healer, both of yourself and of other people. If you feel unwell, start practising these things now, as well as the techniques for healing we have already discussed. You will see that, once you start to take responsibility for yourself, and start using the healing processes we have learned, this change of attitude and lifestyle will aid a faster improvement in your condition. However, remember to be patient.

Looking at your healing skills

Now we will take an active look at how you may wish to start to practise healing on other people. What follows are just suggestions as to the way you may wish to start. Everybody will formulate their own routines and ways of operating, based on the information we have gleaned, so please be aware that what follows are suggestions, not orders.

Before undertaking any healing at all, make sure that you wash your hands in water. Some healers suggest that you should wash your hands in running water (i.e. directly under the tap), but this may not always be possible.

It is important that you are relaxed. Take deep breaths, breathing in and out to a slow count of ten, and trying to breathe in through your nose and out through your mouth, taking in the Universal Power to your body. Do this several times to ensure that you are fully relaxed, as it is easy to transfer your own tension to your patient. Remember, that, unlike self-healing in which you are regenerating your own bodily energy for your own use, with healing other people, you are using the Universal Power from outside of yourself. As we have learned, if you use your own energies to heal others (which is basically pranic healing), you only end up running down your own energy stores, and so become depleted and drained. Pranic healing is, therefore, much better confined to healing yourself rather than others.

It is important to remember that unless you have medical training, you are not a doctor. Do not diagnose. Ask your patient what the problem is, what the symptoms are, and whether a doctor has been consulted and what the diagnosis was. Be aware that sometimes, people are embarrassed about their problem or may find difficulty talking about it. Be patient and don't add any unnecessary pressures.

It is important to make your patients feel at ease, so talk to them, be friendly and help them to feel calm. Explain what spiritual healing is all about (briefly) and explain how you will be using the Universal Power, and that you may be touching them. Make sure they feel comfortable with that, and ascertain whether they believe what you have explained. Explain also that they need to take responsibility for themselves, and maybe, at the end of the session, offer them some guidelines on how they can go about altering their lifestyle, attitudes and emotions. Be sure, however, that you don't lecture your patient.

I would suggest that you ask your patient to sit in a chair, rather than lie down. If you have decided to offer a prayer, this is the time when you should do so, and you can either do this inwardly, or if your patient feels comfortable with the idea, do so aloud.

Some healers suggest that the patients remove their shoes and any spectacles, feeling such things reduce the flow of energy, but again this is up to you.

Stand behind your patient, making sure that neither the arms nor legs are crossed, ask the patient to close the eyes and relax, and with your hands at the level of the patient's head, run your hands through the aura down to the feet, rather than touching the body. See what you feel. Remember that healing needs to work with the aura as well as with the physical body. If you have been practising this technique regularly up to this point, you should be attuned to the different feelings you may experience. You may also wish to see whether you detect any blockages or changes in energy in the chakra centres. Remember that your palms should be towards the patient, with your fingers straight but relaxed, and remember that you are drawing from the Universal Power, so don't try too hard, otherwise you will probably end up with a headache. Just be relaxed, and be aware that you may feel the need to repeat this exercise a few times before moving onwards, so that you are sure of what you are feeling. Some healers, Matthew Manning, for example, will start his healing treatments by placing his hands on the shoulders of his patients, feeling that this helps build up a sense of attunement between patient and healer. However, again this is up to you, and you may wish to try dealing as a first stage with the aura, before moving on to touching your patient.

If you feel that you have a tingling sensation in your fingers when they are over any area, or should you actually be able to see the aura or colour changes, now is the time to concentrate on that area. You may wish at this point to make physical contact with your patient by touch, but again this is up to you. Some people feel happier being touched than others.

All this can take upwards of thirty minutes, and you need to be able to concentrate on the healing for the whole of that time. It is for this reason that, up to this point, we have been practising our own relaxation techniques, because we need to be relaxed. I am fully aware that sometimes, holding your hands in a certain position can make your own muscles ache. I am also aware that sometimes you may find your own mind wandering off. Try to bring your mind back to what you are doing should you find this happening, (you might even like to pray for help at this stage) and remember that if you relax, your own muscle tension will subside.

The healing session should be ended by you running your hands back through the whole aura, from feet up to the head. You may wish to gently put your hands on your patient's shoulders and ask for healing to be continued until your next session, but again this is a personal decision, or you may wish to concentrate a little extra healing on the chakra centre corresponding to the illness that you have been treating.

Be aware of the fact that your patient may feel a little unsteady after a healing session. You may wish to use a few minutes of this 'readjustment time' to explain about affirmations, creative visualisation techniques, changes in lifestyle you recommend, etc. before allowing your patient to stand, but remember that if you have used prayer at the start of the healing, you should also give thanks in prayer at the end of the session. Sometimes, you may find that your patients want to talk about things they felt or experienced. Make sure that you take the time to listen. Sometimes, your patients may have been so relaxed that they found themselves in a meditative state, they may have subconsciously found themselves on a creative visualisation or what to them might have seemed like a bit of a daydream. If your patient doesn't want to talk about the healing session, don't force it. It is their prerogative, one way or the other.

You may wish to explain that the healing you have given is just the start, and that you would recommend further healing treatment. Again, don't force this on someone, but explain that it takes time for an illness to develop, and an equal time for an illness to be treated. Do, however, reinforce the idea that the patient needs to help him or herself as well as allowing you to help through the Universal Power.

I feel it incorrect to charge people for healing. The motivation of healers should be to help other people, not to use other people's illness for their own personal gain. There is far too much emphasis placed on material gain, and many healers feel that the matter of money will hinder the feeling on unconditional love which exists between patient and healer. If people wish to give money, you may wish to suggest that they make a donation to a local or national charity instead.

Remember that the techniques described above are not the only way that people who regularly give healing work. Many people work out

their own routines and ways of healing, and you may also find your own way of working.

When you start to heal other people, you may come across people whose illness or symptoms do not respond to your healing. Please don't assume that you are either doing something wrong or that you are a total failure. Some people will not respond to healing, as we have discussed earlier. Often, the healing will not take effect until after a few sessions anyway. Remember, though, that all you have tried to do is help them. Maybe they have been unwilling to help themselves. Maybe they really don't want to get better, and have a negative attitude about themselves and about any healing being given to them. Perhaps they are expecting too much from the healing you have given. People who are in pain often cannot grade the level of pain they are in, and will says things haven't improved when, in fact, that is not the case. Likewise, someone with mobility problems may not receive a dramatic improvement in their movements, and so feel let down. Please don't give up because you are aware that people aren't seeing dramatic and/or immediate improvements. British healer Matthew Manning finds that sometimes people are not helped by his treatments and suggests to patients that they try another healer. Sometimes, someone else may be able to help where he has failed, so this is another avenue you could suggest, should you find yourself faced with such a problem case.

Conversely, should people see dramatic improvements in their condition, try to remain detached from it all, and don't take the credit for the success. You have merely helped, and are not a miracle worker. Also, you should remember to give thanks in prayer, if you are happy with the concept of prayer.

Another thing of which you should be aware is that sometimes the patient will feel worse after a healing session for a short time. It is not unknown for a patient to start to feel quite nauseous anything up to forty-eight hours after a healing treatment, and you may wish to advise your patients of this. Alternatively, you may prefer not to discuss this unless it happens, in which case you should tell your patient that this is quite natural in some people, and is nothing to worry about. Likewise, on the rare occasions that someone is

actually in the same room with the patient during a healing (say a partner, friend or spouse), sometimes that other person will feel unwell. Again, this is nothing to worry about, and you should seek to reassure the person concerned.

During the course of this chapter, we have covered many aspects of healing, both of self and of others. You may wish to read certain sections on self-healing again before continuing to our final chapter, as I feel it important that we all try to reduce our own problems, before even considering embarking on helping others. It is also important to keep practising your own techniques for visualisation, affirmation, relaxation and stress reduction. You need to be totally relaxed yourself before healing others, and it is well worth taking the time and trouble to practise relaxation techniques as well as creative visualisation when in a relaxed environment.

FINDING A HEALER

Finding a reputable healer can be a difficult task, and should you wish to find one, either for yourself or for other people, you may have difficulty knowing where to start. In the Appendix at the end of this book is a list of organisations that may be able to help you to find a healer. This list is not confined to spiritual healing, and it is not an exhaustive list by any stretch of the imagination, and there are many healers working locally who you may wish to try first. Some healers do advertise in their local papers, and those who feel happy visiting a spiritualist church may find at least one spiritual healing group working from the church each week, normally on the same day and time. If you know of people who have visited a certain healer with good results, you may wish to try visiting that healer. I certainly feel that those with a good reputation are worth a visit as a first point of call. It is also worthwhile thinking about visiting other complementary therapists, especially if you know yourself that some of the health problems you are experiencing are related to either stress or lifestyle difficulties. Included within the Appendix are various organisations of this nature for you to consider. This is all part of helping yourself.

ABSENT HEALING

We briefly mentioned absent healing when we were discussing the power of prayer. I actively pray for those people I know who are ill, either in body or in mind, and firmly believe that this will help them to get better. Remembering that prayer is not confined to specific

distances, the people need not even be aware of the fact that you are praying for them, but they may tell you that they have started to feel better. Likewise, group prayers to people who are absent will have a beneficial effect, due in no small part to the power of energy created by the group.

If you wish to try absent healing, I would advise that you envisage the person concerned in perfect health, and you may also wish to imagine him or her surrounded by a white healing light. If working in a group situation for absent healing, you may wish to have someone sitting in a chair, representative of the absent person being healed. Some people feel this works well. All those taking part in the absent healing should stand around the chair, a relaxed atmosphere should be paramount, and you may wish to have some soothing background music playing.

If those people who are in the group wish to nominate one of the party to hold their hands over the volunteer person acting as the absent party, and offer a prayer, this can add to the power of the session. All those in the group should either concentrate on the person needing healing by saying the person's name or concentrate on a visual image, either actual or mental, of the person concerned.

This takes only a matter of a few minutes, but much has been achieved by those who actively practise absent healing on behalf of their patients.

The benefit of contact

When you were a child and fell over and hurt yourself, maybe you ran to your mother and cried. She would put her hands on the area of concern, and 'rub it better'. Maybe she also said things like 'I'm going to count to ten, and when I've finished, it will be all better'. If you think back to what we have learned, all your mother was actually doing was demonstrating healing – by touch and by affirmation. Therapeutic touch is merely touching an area where there is a problem, transferring the energies to the person, and correcting the

imbalance. This treatment, which is practised extensively in the USA by trained nurses, ideally should be done in a situation of quiet. Dr Dolores Krieger, who was until relatively recently a professor of nursing at New York University, has actively sought to promote the need for people to touch each other, and nurses trained in therapeutic touch have reported many physical improvements in their patients. Tests carried out over a four-year period with a thousand patients at the Neurosurgery clinics of Wisconsin and Minnesota have shown that 90 per cent who received the healing treatment known as Therapeutic Touch were off drugs when they left, while 80 per cent had anything from 50 per cent to 100 per cent relief at the end of the programme.

As we have already pointed out, some people don't like to be touched. We probably all have friends who are 'touchy people'. I have one close friend who loves to give people hugs, irrespective of whether he knows them very well or not. Some people react better to this than others, but at the end of the day, I think that it is important to retain the element of contact between ourselves. As I pointed out earlier, there is certain research which suggest that physical contact can actually prolong our lives.

Research carried out by psychologists has shown that newborn babies who are premature and who are deprived of touch at an early stage may develop problems as a result of the lack of contact. Even hugging a teddy bear has been shown to be better than hugging nothing at all. Likewise, children who are born prematurely and deprived of physical contact from their mothers may have difficulty themselves showing physical affection for other people.

Contact between people is a vital part of a healthy and happy lifestyle, but many people continue to have a problem with touch. There are many therapies you could try which all include the element of touch, and if you are happy to accept that you also have a responsibility to yourself to remain healthy or to regain your health, you may wish to consider various other complementary treatments.

Massage is a particularly good way to promote relaxation, and if you are happy with being touched, I suggest that you consider having a regular massage. Aromatheraphy and reflexology massages combine

the wonderfully relaxing and therapeutic benefits from oils, practitioners of Rolfing will combine an element of psychotherapy with massage, while Shiatsu will combine massage with acupressure techniques, and acupuncture and accupressure themselves will deal directly with the body's natural meridians. Practitioners of metamorphic technique will use manipulation of the feet, but also of the head, hands and neck areas to aid with health problems. Those people suffering from back problems or problems directly related to musculo-skeletal disorders may wish to think about visiting a practitioner of Alexander Technique, or having chiropractic treatment or osteopathic treatment. A visit to a naturopath or hydrotherapist may reinforce the necessity to take responsibility for your own health. Likewise, you may wish to consider a visit to a herbalist, homeopath or practitioner of Bach Flower Remedies, which are now freely available at many outlets.

Those people who suffer badly from stress-related problems may wish to consider looking for a Gestalt therapist, someone qualified in bioenergetics, autogenics, biofeedback or yoga. Alternatively, you may wish to consider experimenting yourself with the power of music, as it is well documented and accepted that music can produce a strong emotional response, and is often used with handicapped children who may have emotional or personal difficulties. Many practitioners of meditation actively use music to enhance guided imagery exercises.

Lifestyle changes for positive health improvements

If we all became reasonably proficient ourselves at learning the art of relaxation, perhaps visits to outside agencies would not be necessary. Likewise, if we acknowledged the problems that our lifestyle was causing, maybe we would do something to prevent many of them. Those of us who work with computers or VDUs, for instance, should

try to work for no longer than two hours without a break, and ideally work for two hours and then have an hour off. I appreciate that this is not always possible, especially where employers are concerned, but if more people realised the link between their lifestyles and their health, maybe the rate of absenteeism through illness would be reduced – employers, please note. Likewise, those employers who actively seek to provide properly balanced nutritional meals in their canteens, and who provide the opportunity for their workforce to have an exercise programme as part of their working day have noticed an improvement in the health of employees and, as a result, an improvement in productivity. Those people working with Japanese companies may already know of the exercises which are encouraged prior to the working day.

Happiness

Most people will agree that when we are happy, things don't seem so bad – even if we aren't well, if someone makes us laugh, we feel a little better. Laughter is an important component in a balanced and healthy life. Matthew Manning has often acknowledged that his patients report an improvement in their conditions when they practise breathing exercises, yoga, mental imagery and laughter.

Laughter, or 'internal jogging' often provides us with contact which we need, and of which we may be deprived if, for example, we live alone and so have limited opportunities for actual physical contact.

Scientists acknowledge that when we laugh we actually take in more oxygen than is normally the case when we merely breathe. Thus we stimulate the circulation, our heart rate increases, and our bodies secrete beneficial hormones. A really good laugh can also cause us to relax, and relaxation is paramount to a healthy lifestyle, reducing tension, stress and depression. If we come closer to understanding that 'We are what we think' as well as 'We are what we eat', we will be a lot more relaxed as a society. As Shakespeare said 'Nothing is good nor bad, but thinking makes it so'.

Psychologists readily admit that those people who are able to laugh, both at themselves and at or with other people, are less likely to suffer from emotional problems than those who can't, especially those who can't laugh at themselves. If we could all try a little harder to be less serious and to 'chill out', maybe we would all feel better as a result. We all need to try harder to share our feelings, to communicate effectively and have fun. I often think that if we could all retain that part of our youth which allowed us 'to be' rather than having demands thrust upon us, by ourselves, our lifestyles and/or our friends and families, we would all be a lot happier.

A friend of mine regularly tells his clients that even a false smile can make you feel better, and then goes on to explain that the muscles in the face, when exercised by either a smile or by laughter, actually benefit and a possible reduction in future wrinkles may result. Whether this is true or not I'm not sure, but at least it makes people smile and/or laugh, so give it a try!

Returning briefly to the power of love, if you are in a relationship with someone, irrespective of whether it is that of parent/child, husband/wife or whatever, please try to tell that person that you love them every now and again and give them a hug. Just knowing that someone cares for you can make you feel happier about yourself and your situation. Those who live alone may wish to look at themselves in the mirror each morning, and say 'I love you'. Silly as it may seem, loving yourself is equally important as being loved by someone else, although the contact and closeness of the other party may be missing. Knowing that you are loved, even by yourself, can go a long way to improving the quality of your life and see an improvement in your general state of wellbeing.

It isn't always possible, but do try to enjoy your life – enjoy what you are doing and do what you enjoy. Happiness is all about being content with your life and your lifestyle. We all need to make sure that we make the most of our time on this planet, and with more awareness of our needs and our responsibilities towards ourselves and others, we will all be more content as a result. 'You are your own boss.' By that, I mean that you should take responsibility for yourself, not that you should be hard on yourself, as being overly demanding of ourselves and others will have a detrimental effect on our health. Usually, all we

really need to do is to improve our own self-image, stop invalidating ourselves and stop being negative.

During the course of this book, we have seen that the healing of mind, body and spirit all begins with ourselves. Spiritual healing is something which we can all do ourselves, for ourselves, with practice, the right attitude and the correct techniques. It is not something which is confined to helping other people, although helping other people to help themselves, as well as helping them by practising spiritual healing is a most worthwhile experience. However, practice is very important, and I really cannot stress enough the need for you to learn to relax and to practise what you are intending to preach to others. Not only will they benefit, but so will you. The aim behind this book is to give you sufficient information to arouse your interest, for you to then move forwards to further knowledge and understanding. Remember, knowledge comes first, understanding follows behind, and we may never have all the answers.

I sincerely hope that the information within this book will have given you things to work towards, as well as things on which you may dwell. Further research and the quest for further knowledge may, hopefully, follow. Even if this is not the case for you, do try to actively work on the guidelines I have outlined, practise the exercises and techniques, develop your own techniques and maintain a positive outlook, even in the face of adversity.

May good health and happiness be yours, always.

Appendix

Organisatons you may wish to contact for further information:

UK

Alexander Technique (STAT)
10 London House
266 Fulham Road
London SW10 9EL

Dr Edward Bach Centre
Mount Vernon
Sotwell
Wallingford
Oxon OX10 0PZ

The British Acupuncture Society
34 Alderney Street
London SW1V 4EU

The British Alliance of Healing
  Associations
Baytrees
47 Beltinge Road
Herne Bay
Kent CT6 6DA

British Touch for Health
  Association
8 Railey Mews
London NW5 2PA

College of Healing
3 Runnings Park
Croft Bank
West Malvern
Worcs WR14 4BP

Gestalt Centre
64 Warwick Road
St Albans
Herts AL1 4DL

The International Rolf Institute
PO Box 1868
Boulder
Colorado 80306
USA

Metamorphic Association
67 Ritherdon Road
London SW17 8QE

National Federation of
  Spiritual Healers
Old Manor Farm Studio
Church Street
Sunbury on Thames
Surrey TW16 6RF

Natural Health Network
Chardstock House
Chard
Somerset TA20 ₂TL

Radionic Association
16A North Bar
Banbury
Oxon OX16 0TF

The Shiatsu Society
14 Oakdene Road
Redhill
Surrey RH1 6BT

Silva Foundation
BCM Self Management
London WC1 3XX

Australia

National Association of ASHA
Gerry Terati Lyons
PO Box 9187
Alice Springs
N T 0871

National Frederation of
 Healers Inc
PO Box 112
Oxenford
Queensland 4210

US

National Spiritualist Association
 of Churches (NSAC)
PO Box 217
Lily Dale
NY 14752 – 0217

Association of Therapeutic
 Healers
Suite 51
67/69 Chancery Lane
London WC2 1AF

White Eagle Lodge
New Lands
Brewells Lane
Rake
Liss
Hampshire GU33 7HY

Canada

National Federation of Spiritual
 Healers (Canada) Inc
TH 64/331
Military Trail
West Hill
Scarborough
Ontario M13 4E3

Ontario Healers Network
390 Queens Quay West
Apartment 2102
Toronto
Ontario M5V 3AG

Association of Spiritual Healers
 of Alberta
Mr J Thomas
40 Edenwold Green N.W.
Calgary
Alberta T3A 5BA

fURTbER READING

Kristyna Arcarti, *Gems and Crystals for beginners*, Headway, 1994

Association for Research and Enlightenment, *An Edgar Cayce Health Anthology*, ARE Press, Virginia Beach, 1979

Edward Bach, *Heal Thyself*, CW Daniel Co, Ltd., 1931

Barbara Ann Brennan, *Hands of Light: A Guide to Healing through the Human Energy Field*, Bantam, London 1988

Hugh Lynn Cayce, *Edgar Cayce on Diet & Health*, Paperback Library, New York, 1969

Dr Larry Dossey, *Healing Words, the Power of Prayer*, Harper, San Francisco, 1993

Harry Edwards, *The Power of Spiritual Healing*, Herbert Jenkins, London, 1963 — *The Healing Intelligence*, Hawthorne, New York, 1965 — *A guide to the Understanding and Practice of Spiritual Healing*, Healer Publishing, 1974

David Lawson, *I See Myself in Perfect Health*, Thorsons, 1994

Naomi Ozaniec, *Chakras for beginners*, Headway, 1994 — *Dowsing for beginners*, Headway, 1994

Tom Pilgrim, *Autobiography of a spiritualist healer*, Sphere Books, 1982

Keith Sherwood, *The Art of Spiritual Healing*, Llewellyn, St Paul, 1985

Pauline Wills, *Visualisation for beginners*, Headway, 1995

Ambrose and Olga Worrall, *The Gift of Healing*, Rider, London, 1969

Other titles in this series

Chakras 0 340 62082 X   The body's energy centres, the chakras, can act as gateways to healing and increased self-knowledge. This book shows you how to work with chakras in safety and with confidence.

Chinese Horoscopes 0 340 64804 X   In the Chinese system of horoscopes, the *year* of birth is all-important. *Chinese Horoscopes for beginners* tells you how to determine your own Chinese horoscope, what personality traits you are likely to have, and how your fortunes may fluctuate in years to come.

Dowsing 0 340 60882 X   People all over the world have used dowsing since the earliest times. This book shows how to start dowsing – what to use, what to dowse, and what to expect when subtle energies are detected.

Dream Interpretation 0 340 60150 7   This fascinating introduction to the art and science of dream interpretation explains how to unravel the meaning behind dream images to interpret your own and other people's dreams.

Feng Shui 0 340 62079 X   This beginner's guide to the ancient art of luck management will show you how to increase your good fortune and well-being by harmonising your environment with the natural energies of the earth.

Gems and Crystals 0 340 60883 8   For centuries gems and crystals have been used as an aid to healing and meditation. This guide tells you all you need to know about choosing, keeping and using stones to increase your personal awareness and improve your well-being.

Graphology 0 340 60625 8   Graphology, the science of interpreting handwriting to reveal personality, is now widely accepted and used throughout the world. This introduction will enable you to make a comprehensive analysis of your own and other people's handwriting to reveal the hidden self.

Herbs for Magic and Ritual 0 340 67415 6   This introduction to the lore of herbs and their properties gives simple ways to activate your own healing and magical abilities.

I Ching 0 340 62080 3   The roots of *I Ching* or the *Book of Changes* lie in the time of the feudal mandarin lords of China, but its traditional wisdom is still relevant today. Using the original poetry in its translated form, this introduction traces its history, survival and modern-day applications.

Love Signs 0 340 64805 8   This is a practical introduction to the astrology of romantic relationships. It explains the different roles played by each of the planets, focusing particularly on the position of the Moon at the time of birth.

Meditation 0 340 64835 X   This beginner's guide gives simple, clear instructions to enable you to start meditating and benefiting from this ancient mental discipline immediately. The text is illustrated throughout by full-colour photographs and line drawings.

Numerology 0 340 59551 5   Despite being scientifically based, numerology requires no great mathematical talents to understand. This introduction gives you all the information you will need to understand the significance of numbers in your everyday life.

Paganism 0 340 67013 4   Pagans are true Nature worshippers who celebrate the cycles of life. This guide describes pagan festivals and rituals and takes a detailed look at the many forms of paganism practised today.

Palmistry 0 340 59552 3   Palmistry is the oldest form of character reading still in use. This illustrated guide shows you exactly what to look for and how to interpret what you find.

Runes 0 340 62081 1   The power of the runes in healing and giving advice about relationships and life in general has been acknowledged since the time of the Vikings. This book shows how runes can be used in our technological age to increase personal awareness and stimulate individual growth.

Star Signs 0 340 59553 1   This detailed analysis looks at each of the star signs in turn and reveals how your star sign affects everything about you. This book shows you how to use this knowledge in your relationships and in everyday life.

Tarot 0 340 59550 7   Tarot cards have been used for many centuries. This guide gives advice on which sort to buy, where to get them and how to use them. The emphasis is on using the cards positively, as a tool for gaining self-knowledge, while exploring present and future possibilities.

The Moon and You 0 340 64836 8   The phase of the Moon when you were born radically affects your personality. This book looks at nine lunar types – how they live, love, work and play, and provides simple tables to find out the phase of your birth.

Visualisation 0 340 65495 3   This introduction to visualisation, a form a self-hypnosis widely used by Buddhists, will show you how to practise the basic techniques – to relieve stress, improve your health and increase your sense of personal well-being.

Witchcraft 0 340 67014 2   This guide to the ancient religion based on Nature worship answers many of the questions and uncovers the myths and misconceptions surrounding witchcraft. Mystical rituals and magic are explained and there is advice for the beginner on how to celebrate the sabbats.